ORDERING FROM THE COSMIC KITCHEN

"Here is a clear, practical, wisdom-filled guide to bringing your life into harmony with your heart's desires. Put these principles into practice, and you are sure to find what you are looking for. These affirmations really work!"

Alan Cohen
Best-selling author of
The Dragon Doesn't Live Here Anymore

"If you're ready to lovingly nurture yourself with positive affirmations, here's the book for you."

Mark Victor Hansen
Co-creator, #1 *New York Times* best-selling series
Chicken Soup for the Soul®

"There are three parts to a recipe: ingredients, method, and result. In this little recipe book, you will find all three. Simple ingredients, a practical method, and an amazing result. But the "cherry on top" is Patricia's charming way of mixing it all together. You will love this tasty morsel!"

Barbara Mark & Trudy Griswold
Best-selling authors of the *Angelspeake* books

"If you're hungry for a more fulfilling life, this is the book for you. All that is good, true and beautiful is ready to be placed on your table when you decide what you want. Dr. Crane shows you what's on the menu, how to effectively place your order, and why the Great Universal Chef never fails to prepare only the finest sustenance for your particular taste."

John Randolph Price
Best-selling author and
Chairman of the Quartus Foundation

ORDERING FROM THE COSMIC KITCHEN:

The Essential Guide to Powerful, Nourishing Affirmations

Patricia J. Crane, Ph.D.

The Crane's Nest

Bonsall, California

Published by:
The Crane's Nest, a division of Health Horizons.
P.O. Box 1486
Bonsall, California, 92003
(800) 969–4584
www.heartinspired.com

ISBN: 1–893705–15–3
Revised edition
Self Help/Inspirational

Dedication

This book is dedicated to all those who are
seeking to make positive changes in their own
lives and to help our planet.

Acknowledgments

Although this book was written in only a few months, the "incubation" period lasted for years as I was guided to all the experiences necessary to put these ideas on paper.

First I wish to thank Spirit for all the expressions of the Divine who have been a part of my spiritual growth. They include: Rev. Dr. Carol Lawson, Rev. Peggy Bassett, Rev. Terry Cole–Whittaker, Deepak Chopra, M.D., Alan Cohen, Louise Hay, Richard Moss, M.D., Brugh Joy, M.D., Jean Houston, Ph.D., Marianne Williamson, and Abraham, among many others.

I am greatly appreciative to family, friends and colleagues who have supported me, particularly during the last two years: Mary Anne Block, Anita Brown, Steve and Ingrid Crane, Chip and Linda Crane, Rev. Doug Fogelsong, Victoria Jordan, Karen McKee, Bill Mayo, Judith–Annette Milburn, Ph.D., Sue Minkin, Karen and Lew Pulley, Blair Rice, Earl and Janet Rogers, and Stef Swink. I thank all the members of the Inside Edge for their love, enthusiasm, and inspiration, particularly Odile Nicolette.

Words are not adequate to express the gratitude I feel for all the workshop leaders I have trained who have taken the ideas in this book to thousands of people in over thirty countries. Your letters, calls, and emails have touched me deeply. You are contributing so much to the healing of this planet. Thank you to those of you who contributed stories for this book. My deepest gratitude to Norma Jarvis, who has organized my workshops so wonderfully in England since 1991, as well as my main assistants there and in the U.S.: Verity Dawson, Lois Bennett, and Jackie Turner. My thanks also to Heather Williams, whose non–dominant hand work is so powerful. A special salute to Mary Heath, who is sharing this work so beautifully in Australia.

Thanks to my editor, Bobbie Probstein, for her suggestions, enthusiasm, and encouragement.

Finally, to my life partner Rick Nichols: thank you for being my friend, lover, and spiritual partner. You bring such joy and beauty into my life. My heart is so grateful for our relationship and all the support and encouragement you give me. We are, indeed, peanut butter 'n jelly: different, but delicious together.

Introduction

This book is intended to inspire you with a new vision for your life. It includes techniques, particularly affirmations and visualizations, that will empower you to achieve your dreams. I didn't learn these ideas growing up and you probably didn't either. During my teens, I intuitively sensed there was a way to live life differently, but it was years before I discovered what that was. The principles in this book and the stories that illustrate them took me years to learn. It is my hope that by presenting them here, your own learning curve will be shortened!

Welcome to:

The Cosmic Kitchen

Menu..........

All orders served with generous portions of joy, laughter, hope, and love.

Starters

Entrées

Desserts

Whenever you're ready,
the Cosmic Kitchen will take your order.

I am open to new ways of thinking and feeling about life. I now recognize my own responsibility for creating the life of my dreams. I open my arms to embrace life with joy and enthusiasm.

Chapter 1

Your Order, Please!

There are so many restaurants to choose from when you decide to go out to eat. There are fast food drive–thrus, little neighborhood places that have been there for years, chains, and elegant ones atop buildings that look out over the expanse of a city. Take a minute to remember the last time you went to a restaurant. What kind was it? What kind of service did you receive? How varied was the menu? Did you order what you wanted regardless of the price? When you ordered, did you worry about whether or not you would actually get the food?

This book will demonstrate to you that the Universe is like an infinite Cosmic Kitchen, and there is a Cosmic Chef waiting to fulfill YOUR orders. The key is knowing what you want and how to place your order. So grab a cup of tea from your own kitchen (or other favorite beverage), sit in a comfortable chair, and get ready to create your own orders from the Cosmic Kitchen!

Most of us grew up thinking that life was random. Some good things happen and some challenges happen, but you can't control them. That's certainly how it was for me. We were an average middle–class family in New Jersey. Both my parents were left–brained accountants. I learned to believe that you could have nice things, but not what you REALLY wanted because what you really wanted was too expensive. Of course, I was also taught that studying hard would result in good grades (it did) and that being nice to people would result in having friends (it did). What I wasn't taught was how my <u>thoughts</u> are continually creating my experience. I wasn't taught that there is a Law of Attraction that is constantly operating. I learned this lesson in a most unusual way.

During my late twenties I worked for a county welfare office in Los Angeles. It was a very stressful job because all the county workers were caught between doing their best to help people and the administrative rules that governed everything. And it didn't help that the general public held negative attitudes about people on welfare. Being a perfectionist (I am now recovering) I did my best to please everyone, turning in the volumes of paperwork on time and listening compassionately to the clients in my caseload.

After a few years, the work was taking its toll on me physically and emotionally. I seemed to run on cigarettes and caffeine and never felt rested even after a lot of sleep. A doctor prescribed Valium, but that barely made a dent in my anxiety level. One day I walked into the office, impulsively wrote out my resignation for two weeks hence and put it on my supervisor's desk. Although she did her best to change my mind, I was determined to leave and recover my sanity.

OK, so now I'm at home, the home I share with my boyfriend, who also works at the welfare office and who is also on Valium. Over the next few months while he's working at the welfare department, I spend a lot of time watching the Watergate hearings (the best soap opera ever), making ceramics for a small business I started, and mulling over what the hell is life all about? My Valium prescription ended, but the anxiety didn't. So, I started having a glass of wine to help the anxiety, than another and another. Soon I was drinking my first glass of wine at 10

A.M. in the morning. I never got drunk; I just drank enough to medicate the anxiety. Inside, I was screaming out for help. What I didn't realize at the time was that my cry for help had gone to the Cosmic Kitchen and help was on its way, right to my own front door.

The help arrived in an unexpected way. One evening an adorable young black boy rang my doorbell. He smiled and handed me a little flyer and said "you're invited to a lecture" and then turned and skipped away. I looked at the flyer—the lecture was at his home, just down the street, and it was on meditation. Have you ever had one of those bells go off in your mind, when you just KNOW something is right? Well, the bell in my head was deafening! I immediately called his mom and said I'd be there.

The person giving the lecture that Wednesday was in his late twenties, with short hair, and dressed in a suit. Given this was the seventies, his look was definitely not one most men his age had in those days. He talked about the benefits of meditation, and how people were less stressed and more productive. He told his own story about how it had allowed him to heal an ulcer that even medication hadn't helped. I had been convinced that I wanted to start meditating before I even attended the lecture, but now I couldn't wait to get started! I signed up to start the classes that very Saturday.

The atmosphere at the meditation center was strange to me. There was incense burning and an altar with flowers and fruit on a table. It was very quiet and peaceful though, and I liked that. I was soon instructed in this very simple technique and left feeling refreshed and—more important—really happy. Something profound had happened. The colors of the sky and the trees and the flowers seemed incredibly vibrant as I drove home. In the core of my being, I knew life had changed forever. I began practicing the technique faithfully twice a day for about 15 minutes each time. Over the next few weeks I attended some classes with my instructor and several other people who had just started meditating. We all reported positive effects on our lives. Within two weeks I had cut my smoking in half and was only drinking a glass of wine a day. I was truly amazed. After a few more weeks, I wasn't drinking at all. My energy was up, my anxiety down, and life was looking beautiful!

Then I looked at my checkbook and realized it was almost empty. Although the idea of going back to the welfare department wasn't thrilling, it was the easiest because there were always job openings available. The next day I called the hiring department and discovered they had an opening near my home, supervising the same type of unit I had supervised before. Within a week I was working in the welfare department again, but now it seemed really different. My whole world had shifted just because of a simple meditation technique. And, coincidentally (I now believe there are no coincidences because they are all planned by the Cosmic Coordinator), the wife of my instructor worked there, as did a few others who meditated. We started meeting early before work to practice the technique together.

Despite the fact that I had returned to the welfare department, my heart wanted a different career. So I enrolled in psychology classes at the local university at night (I already had my bachelor's degree with double majors in biology and chemistry.) Despite working all day and taking classes and studying every night, I felt great. I felt great, but my partner didn't. He was always complaining about how tired he was, how stressed, blah, blah, blah. I was so excited that meditation had helped me, I couldn't understand why he wouldn't try it. Finally, I found a small apartment and moved out by myself.

Within a year, I had started another job as a vocational rehabilitation counselor working for the state. I was still finishing my psychology units so that I could apply for graduate school in psychology. My life was full and exciting and happy. I was dating (OK, living with a man I met through my work. Hey—remember it's the seventies.)

I began noticing that I would think about

things and they would happen. Some of them were small, like thinking about someone and the person would call me or we would run into each other in the grocery store. Lots of people experience things like that. But others were more significant. The rehab unit where I worked also led training programs for other counselors from around the state. I found myself really wanting a part–time position in the training unit so that I could take more units at the university and be able to apply for graduate school quickly. However, I had only been there a short time AND there were no part–time positions. Within a few months, one of the trainers quit. The administrator decided to make the position part–time, and it was mine!

I still thought this was a nice coincidence, but in reality the Cosmic Kitchen was responding to the order I had sent out.

During my last semester at the undergraduate level, I spotted a class called "Assertiveness Training" and knew I needed to take it. It was an exciting class in communication skills taught by a professor and an assistant. It felt really powerful to be using the techniques from the class to change my life in even more positive ways. I particularly liked the idea that the way we talk to ourselves, self–talk, is critical in how we handle things in life. If we say to ourselves "I can't" then we can't. If we say to ourselves,

"It's too hard to do that" it is. If we think about situations in negative ways, then the solution can't present itself. As I practiced better self–talk, I felt calmer. Then I began thinking about how much fun it would be to teach this class myself. The Cosmic Chef went to work. At the end of the class, the assistant called me and said he needed a co–teacher for his community college assertiveness class. Was I interested? Are you kidding? But I didn't have a teaching credential for the community colleges. Usually, at least a master's degree is required, and I hadn't even started graduate school. Not to worry. As it turned out, I could apply to have a specialty credential because of completing the assertiveness class at the university.

Now it's September, 1976, and I'm recently married, in a new house and community, teaching at a community college, and starting graduate school in a Ph.D. program in social psychology. Whew! I started meditating even more to keep some balance. Graduate school was exciting and scary, because I had always thought of myself as smart, but not brilliant (limiting thought), so I did adequately in the program, but wasn't outstanding. My best classes the first year were in computer programming and statistics— must be those genes from my parents, the two accountants.

Toward the end of the first year, I discovered

that there was a teaching assistant position open for the statistics class. For some reason, I found myself REALLY wanting it, but despite taking the assertiveness class, I was never able to approach the professor about the job. During the last week of class, the professor asked me and two other students to stay after class to talk with him. I went into shock as he spoke. He said that all of us had applied for the teaching assistant position, and he had decided to offer it to me. He thanked the other two and they left. I have no memory of anything I said to him, as my head was reeling. How did this happen? I had never even spoken to him about the position!

I drove home in bewilderment and told my husband what had happened. My thoughts had manifested before, but this was different. The professor actually thought I had spoken to him about the position, when I knew I hadn't. I realized I needed to understand what was going on. Without consciously knowing it, that order too went to the Cosmic Kitchen.

The order was filled in the form of a book called *Seth Speaks* by Jane Roberts. The wisdom in the book was "channeled" through Jane Roberts from a non-physical entity named Seth. I had never heard of anything like this before, and thought it very bizarre, but somehow the message in the book resonated with me. Another bell went off inside. This book told me that we each create our own reality. The concept was at once familiar and strange. But the more I read, the more I knew it was true. I began to wonder why no one had told me this growing up. Didn't they know?

My search led me to other resources and other books. I learned about affirmations and visualization and realized I had been practicing these techniques for years without knowing it. I seemed especially good at manifesting new jobs. Now that I understood the techniques, I could start using them consciously in all areas of my life.

Because you have this book in your hand, you must be ready to more consciously place your own orders with the Cosmic Kitchen. Take a few minutes to think about some of the events in your life up until now and how you placed your orders without knowing it. Some of these orders you may have judged as "good" and others as "bad." It doesn't matter. Right now you're gaining awareness about how you have created YOUR reality up until now. Write down some of your previous orders on the last page of this chapter.

In the next chapter, we'll start with the basics for ordering.

My Orders Up Until Now.....

In this moment, I choose to believe that I deserve a wonderful life. I lovingly notice any limiting thoughts and gently weed them from my inner garden. I choose positive, nurturing thought patterns for myself.

Chapter 2

The Basics for Placing Your Order

When you go to a restaurant, do you scan the menu and tell the waiter everything you DON'T want? Do you tell the waitress to get you "anything?" Of course not! You look over the menu, narrow it down to a few choices, and then choose one. (Or, if you are a Libra, you vacillate so long your partner finally chooses for you.)

Principle #1

YOU NEED TO DECIDE WHAT YOU WANT.

You tell the waiter or waitress what you want, and he or she goes off to the kitchen and places the order. Do you sit there and worry about whether you'll get it or how long it will take? Probably not. (Sometimes the waiter does come back and say the kitchen doesn't have that selection, and that's another chapter in the book.) You TRUST that the chef and the staff in the kitchen are responding to your order in the best way they can. However, deciding what you really want in life can be more challenging than going into a real restaurant because the Menu of Life is infinite, while restaurants usually specialize in a particular kind of food and have a limited menu. At the end of this chapter there is a page for you to write down your orders to the Cosmic Kitchen. Be as expansive and outrageous as you want to be.

It's also important to be SPECIFIC about what you want. My friend Norma in England started affirming for job interviews—and she got *them*, but no job. She needed to be affirming for a successful interview that would lead to her being offered a wonderful job.

Principle #2

COSMIC KITCHEN ORDERS ARE POSITIVE, PRESENT TENSE, AND PERSONAL.

State your affirmations as though they have already happened. Say "I have.... I receive.... I am...." And so on. If you state your affirmations in the future tense (I will have....) they will stay in the future, rather than manifesting in your present time. State what you DO want, not what you DON'T want. Affirm that "I have a wonderful new job" rather than "I want to get out of this place." Or, "My body is vibrant and healthy" rather than "I'm no longer sick."

The Law of Attraction brings you what you focus on. √ If you're experiencing a health challenge, yet continually thinking about how sick you are and that you'll never get well, you are depressing your body's own healing mechanisms with every negative thought. If your finances are low and you continually think about how little money you have and send out a message of fear to the Cosmic Kitchen, you won't be able to receive the good the Universe wants to give you.

If you're reading this and thinking, "But how can I think positively when the reality is that I AM sick, or I AM about to file bankruptcy, or my job IS terrible?" You're right—it's not easy to have faith when you're in the midst of challenge. What have you got to lose? Start by thinking, "What do I want?" At the end of this chapter there is a page for you to start writing your affirmations. You can also go to the chapters on specific topics like health and prosperity and get some ideas on how to phrase your affirmations. Write them, read them, feel them, and choose to BELIEVE they will work.

Principle #3

INCLUDE WORDS THAT CONVEY POSITIVE, ENERGETIC FEELINGS.

It feels wonderful that..... I am so happy and excited to be..... It is fantastic to..... The more positive energy you can generate with your affirmations, the more quickly they tend to manifest. Sing your affirmations with gusto, dance them with joy. Stand in front of a mirror with your arms outstretched and say your affirmations with enthusiasm!

You may have heard the phrase, "change your thinking, change your life." I would add to that and say, "change your thoughts and feelings and change your life." If you are thinking, "I am deserving of all good," but the message you are sending out with your feelings is "No way," the Universe will respond to your feelings. Along with your positive affirmations, practice FEELING as though they're already true.

Principle #4

TRUST THE TIMING OF DELIVERY. LET GO OF YOUR TIMELINE.

Cosmic orders may require different amounts of preparation. Some have many ingredients that must come together to complete the dish while others have only a few ingredients. Allow the Universe to bring things together at the right moment for you. When you're at a restaurant, do you run to the kitchen every few minutes to check on it? (I know a few of you controlling types would like to!) Most people are content to enjoy talking to the person they're with for dinner, the ambiance of the restaurant, and a glass of wine while waiting.

Have you ever had a fleeting thought and had it manifest? If so, that was an example of putting in an order to the Cosmic Kitchen and then letting it go. One day in the mid–eighties, I thought *I'd really like to do more work with women.* Within a month, I received calls to speak at two women's conferences and a local women's group.

A part of trusting the timing for your order to arrive is letting go of the need to have it. While this may seem paradoxical, if there is an underlying sense of fear when you do your affirmations, the Universe responds to the fear. Let's say your finances are low and you are affirming for money. If the fear that you WON'T receive what you need is stronger than your trust that you WILL, the Universe responds to the feeling of fear, and your good is kept away. Practice feeling a sense of trust, even if your logical mind tells you something different. If you are affirming for a relationship, practice being happy and fulfilled right now. That kind of energy is very attractive.

The stronger the feeling of trust, the more quickly the Chef can complete your order. *A Course in Miracles* tells us that "infinite patience produces immediate results." When you are trusting the timing, you can go about your daily life with joy, knowing that all is well.

Principle #5

LET THE COSMIC CHEF DECIDE HOW YOU RECEIVE YOUR ORDER.

When you do an affirmation and then start imagining how it will happen, that is called "outlining." This is something you want to avoid. The Chef always has the best combination of ingredients to put together for your order. For example, I had completed my master's degree when I started affirming for a teaching job. If I had "outlined", I probably would have called the local community colleges to see what job openings they had. As it happened, the Cosmic Chef arranged for me to teach at the university level, a result that was better than expected, since I had no idea I could teach there without a Ph.D. Once you have created the affirmation that expresses the result you want, focus lightly on the result, not the process to get there. Shakti Gawain, author of *Creative Visualization*, recommends that you add the phrase "this or something better" at the end of your affirmations.

Principle #6

ALLOW YOUR INNER WISDOM TO GUIDE YOU IN THE RIGHT BALANCE BETWEEN ACTION AND ALLOWING.

As you will see from personal stories in this book,

many times I simply said my affirmation for a new job or something else, and it just "fell in my lap." Of course, I had to do the preparation to be ready to do the work, but I didn't do anything to make it happen. Can you just sit and watch TV and eat bon–bons while you wait for the Cosmic Chef to fulfill your order? Well, sometimes....

One of my longtime friends, Sue, is an attractive blonde with lots of energy. So far, she has had three major careers. In one of them, she practiced law. (OK, now, let's have some positive thoughts for the lawyers of the world. They need love, too.) At one point, she wanted to change law firms, and talked to me for months about how she needed to get her résumé together. I could tell by the lack of enthusiasm that she wasn't really looking forward to that task, so I said, "well, maybe you don't. Just tell the Universe what you want." Not too long after that, she received a call that gave her the new position, without having to do a résumé. In her next move, how- ever, it was important for her to put together her résumé.

When you meditate, ask for guidance in any action you are to take to help the Cosmic Kitchen. Listen to that Inner Wisdom. If something feels forced, back off. Affirm that you are perfectly guided in ALL your activi- ties.

Principle #7

BELIEVE THAT YOU DESERVE TO HAVE A WONDERFUL LIFE.

Many people feel they are not entitled to health, wealth, happiness, and a wonderful relationship. The truth is, we are all deserving of all good, but others who didn't feel worthy taught us something different.

What were you taught as a child about having a wonderful life? Are you willing to believe that you DO deserve a fantastic life?

Principle #8

FEEL GRATITUDE TO THE UNIVERSE AND THE COSMIC CHEF FOR FULFILLING YOUR ORDER IN THE MOST MIRACULOUS WAY.

Gratitude is a wonderful feeling at the heart level. It not only sends out positive energy around your affirmations, it also helps you with feeling the trust that it is already being taken care of. Every day take some time to make a gratitude list, either mentally or on paper. Cultivating the "attitude of gratitude" will create wonderful miracles in your life.

Common Questions about Placing Orders:

❖ *Why do affirmations work?*

Affirmations work because your thoughts are not contained in that physical structure we call the brain. We are all connected (yes, all) in Divine Mind, Unlimited Potential, God, whatever you want to call It. Your thoughts, whether they are positive or negative, are an energy that connects to the universal consciousness, the Cosmic Kitchen and Chef, and the Law of Attraction that brings your orders to you. Affirmations are energized even more with positive feelings, so practice FEEL-ING your affirmations as though they are already a reality!

❖ *How many orders can I give the kitchen at any one time?*

Unlike a regular kitchen, the Cosmic Kitchen can handle an infinite number of orders at any one time. It doesn't matter how many other people are putting in their orders or how many you have; it can respond to all of them. The real question is: how many do YOU feel comfortable with? You can write out as many affirmations as you want, and then just allow the Universe to act on them.

❖ *How often do I need to say or think my affirmations?*

When it comes to affirmations, once is actually enough if your belief is strong enough. However, most people find that by saying their affirmations on a daily basis, they reinforce the new beliefs for themselves. Discover what is comfortable for you.

❖ ***How can I check on my order to see if it's really being prepared?***

Please go back and re–read basic principle #4. The operative word here is TRUST. Have you ever gone to the kitchen in a restaurant to check on your order? (OK, so a few of you Type A's have, but most of us are more patient than that.) Pressuring the chef in a restaurant or complaining to the waitress may speed up service, but it doesn't work with the Cosmic Kitchen! There is a timing that is perfect for preparing and delivering your order.

Here's another analogy: when you plant seeds in your garden, you know you need to water, fertilize, and weed around them. You don't go pulling the seeds up every few days to check and see if they're growing. In the same way, you want to lightly think and FEEL that your affirmations are a reality and go about your daily business with joy and trust, because you know that you are always supported by Spirit.

❖ ***Can you do affirmations for others?***

Sometimes. If you and another person agree on an affirmation for her/him, it's OK. For example, your partner is looking for a new job, and you are both affirming, "_____ has the perfect new job," that's fine. Or, you may be affirming with a friend for her vibrant health and vitality. However, you can't try and control others with affirmations. If you have a disagreeable boss, rather than thinking he's found another job, affirm "I always have a good relationship with my boss." Remember to focus on the result you want for yourself.

❖ *Why don't orders always get fulfilled?*

The Law of Attraction always fulfills your orders, even though it may not seem like it. If you don't feel deserving of what you want or you have inconsistent feelings about what you want, the Law of Attraction will give you the order with the strongest feelings. Let's say you are affirming for a new job paying a lot more than you're making right now. But the order isn't completely clear, because you're also thinking you'll have to work a lot harder at the new job, and you don't want to do that. Until you get clear, the new job can't be delivered. You could affirm "I have a fabulous new job making $_____ a year, working less than I do now, and having more fun."

If you're ill and getting well will mean resuming some responsibilities you don't want, you will continue to attract illness. If you are affirming for a relationship, but you're actually fearful of having one, it won't manifest.

When I was administering wellness worksite programs, I thought I would affirm to lead stress reduction programs as a consultant and make a lot of money. It never happened, for two reasons. First of all, the motivation to just "make a lot of money" doesn't fit with my values, and second, I really wanted to share spiritual ideas and my own (limiting) thought was that I couldn't do that in the corporate world. Now, I'm clear that I can offer spiritual principles anywhere, be of service to people wherever I give my programs, and be prosperous.

❖ **Why do some things happen that I DON'T want to happen?**

If you send out a strong message, I DON'T WANT...., it's the same as sending out a strong message I DO WANT.... Try this: Don't think about a pink elephant. The image that immediately pops into your mind is a pink elephant, right? Your unconscious mind doesn't process the "don't." When you say I DON'T, the image of what you don't want goes to the Cosmic Kitchen. Now stay calm—you don't need to start worrying about every random thought. It's the energy and the repetition that are important. Just pay attention to your thoughts and feelings: change the "I don't wants...." to think about what you DO want.

On the next page you'll find some examples of affirmations, and on the last page of this chapter there is a space for you to start writing your orders to the Cosmic Kitchen. Have FUN!

The next chapter has several exercises to help you clear out conflicting beliefs and feelings.

Examples of affirmations:

I am deserving of a wonderful life. I now consciously create the life of my dreams!

❖

I receive an abundance of love from my friends and family.

❖

I love and approve of myself. I am always doing the best I can.

❖

I am healthy, wealthy, and wise.

❖

I'm having a love affair with life!

❖

My body is strong and healthy and every cell is alive with health and energy.

❖

I am delighted to be using my talents and abilities in my ideal career position! I now know and follow the Divine Plan for my life.

❖

I trust my Inner Wisdom, knowing that all the answers are within me.

❖

Did you read these affirmations and feel that you couldn't say some of them for yourself? Then it's time for some clearing out.

My Orders to the Cosmic Kitchen....

Chapter 3

Clearing the Old Menu Items

We all grow up with numerous ideas and beliefs about how life works, what our self–worth is, what abilities we have, how relationships work, whether we deserve money, and so on. As you are creating your affirmations for what you want in life, it's also important to become aware of what you've been ordering up until now, and clear out the menu items you no longer want. Psychologists tell us that most of our ideas about life are in place by the time we are five years old.

Let's take some time to get clear about the old

menu you've been using. Some of the items may be positive and some negative. It's good to identify both. So grab some paper and a pen, put on some relaxing music, and take about twenty minutes to just list the beliefs you took on in childhood about yourself, relationships, money, careers, health, and any other area you can think of. Make two columns, one for the positive beliefs and one for the negative ones that really don't serve you. Not enough time? For right now, just limit the time to twenty minutes because much more could be overwhelming.

Now look over your list. Are there more positives or negatives? Even if there are a lot of negatives, that's OK. You need to be aware before you can make changes.

Several years ago I was leading a two day workshop in London as an AIDS benefit. One of the exercises had the participants tap into their Inner Wisdom and then use that wisdom to assist someone else. As I was guiding the participants through a meditation to get in touch with their Inner Wisdom, two people jumped up and left the room. After finishing the meditation and getting the other participants started on the sharing, I quickly went out to the hallway to speak with the two who had run out. Both of them were feeling really angry. As we talked, what came out was that each of them (unrelated to the other) had been told as a child, "You're stupid!" They grew up believing this, so how could they possibly tap into Inner Wisdom? The tears started as I explained that this was just an old menu item that needed to be cleared. Just like everyone else, they truly did have access to Inner Wisdom. We hugged and returned to the room, where they assisted each other in making a breakthrough.

The "clearing out" process is continual. This is because we go to deeper and deeper levels of the unconscious mind as time goes on. Consider the image of an iceberg. Only a small part of the iceberg is visible above the surface. Throughout our lives, we're continually bringing more of the iceberg (the unconscious beliefs) to the surface. As you become aware of a limiting belief that you no longer want on your menu, you can create an affirmation for the new belief. Take some time right now to go back to your list and begin writing out positive affirmations for the negative beliefs you have identified so far. There is also a page at the end of this chapter you can use. I would really recommend getting a special notebook or journal to use for your affirmations. You can purchase one that is especially attractive to you or make one yourself. You want to have a positive feeling just by looking at your journal, and (at least for me) some yellow lined paper doesn't do it.

Common old menu items for people include:
- ❖ I'm not a lovable person.
- ❖ I don't deserve a great life.
- ❖ I'm not smart enough to be successful.
- ❖ I'm not attractive enough to be acceptable.

❖ There's never enough money.
❖ Relationships are difficult.
❖ I can't have my dream job.
❖ I have to work hard at a job I don't like and not earn what I'm worth.
❖ Health is a matter of genetics and chance.

When these old items are on the menu, the Law of Attraction will continue to bring you experiences that "prove" these old ideas are correct. The old belief is perpetuated and the cycle continues. When you start consciously doing affirmations, these old ideas will have a tendency to want to show up on the menu again, so you need to practice repetition, repetition, <u>repetition</u>, until you get really comfortable with the new menu. Deepak Chopra says that we have about 90,000 thoughts a day and 75,000 of them are the same ones we had yesterday and the day before. And then we wonder why our lives continue in much the same way!

When you first begin making conscious changes in your thoughts, your time for affirmations may seem separate from the rest of your life. However, as you continue practicing, you'll be practicing thinking positive thoughts as often as possible.

Below is an exercise to use to identify your "typical" daily thoughts. I've led thousands of people through this exercise, and even those who have been practicing the ideas in this book for a long time find there are areas where they need to make changes.

Read through the process first and then go back and experience it. Or you can tape it and then play it to yourself.

Take a nice deep breath and close your eyes. Imagine you are just waking up on a typical day in your life....When you first wake up, what are your usual thoughts? Are you grateful to be alive and excited about your day, are you neutral, or are you dreading getting up?.....Now become aware of your thoughts as you get ready for your day (either work or other activities).....What are you thinking?......As you are getting dressed and see yourself in the mirror, how do you react?......What kinds of thoughts do you have as you are commuting to work?....How do you react as you see your coworkers and your boss? Are you judging them or do you know they're doing the best they can?....When you go to lunch, are you worried about the calories or do you feel good about choosing healthy food?....Become aware of your typical thoughts as you continue through your day and go home or to other evening activities.....What are your usual last thoughts as you prepare for bed and go to sleep? Now take a few deep breaths, stretch, and gently bring your awareness back to the room and open your eyes.

31

Did you become aware of thought patterns you need to change? Make some notes on the "typical" thoughts you want to change so that you can create affirmations for them.

Now let's talk about some techniques that help you become aware of the old menu items and clear them out.

Listen to yourself talk:

Really listen. Do you talk about your limitations and why you can't have what you want? Or do you talk about how exciting your life is and the positive expectancies you have? If you're protesting, "but my life ISN'T wonderful right now," guess what? You are continuing that belief for yourself. In the beginning it takes a LOT of awareness to focus on what you DO want, but the results are worth the energy. It's YOUR life. You can decide it's a joy rather than a drudge at any moment! Get it? YOU DECIDE! When I listen to people, I often hear the words "I'm stuck" or "I can't seem to get past this issue." The words the person is thinking and saying keep them stuck. How can the Universe give you an insight if you keep saying you're stuck? The Law of Attraction always works. It simply responds to what you are thinking and speaking. Affirm that you have the awareness you need to shift to a new level. Affirm that you are speaking in positive and expansive ways about your life.

Try the clustering technique:

To use the clustering technique you take a blank piece of paper and write a topic in the center of it with a circle around it. You might write "what I believe about myself" or "money and material things" or "relationships" or "my perfect career." Then you quickly write as many associations as you can around the topic. Do this quickly so you don't start thinking logically about it. After about ten minutes, stop and review what you've written and then start creating affirmations for the associations you want to change. For example, if "money and material things" was in the center and one of the ideas you wrote was "never enough," then you would write out an affirmation like: "I ALWAYS have enough money to pay my bills ahead of time and have plenty left over for fun."

Use the mirror technique:

Say your affirmations to yourself looking into a mirror, really looking into your own eyes. Especially say positive affirmations about loving and approving of yourself and how deserving you are. Popularized by author Louise Hay in her best-selling book *You Can Heal Your Life*, many people have found this technique provides a quantum leap in feeling good about themselves and enhances their self-esteem. While in private practice, I always used the mirror technique in the first session. Somehow this technique touches the inner self very quickly, and often the first response is tears as the person looks at her/himself deeply for the first time. Many couldn't say to themselves "I love you" right away, so we started with "I am willing to love and approve of you." As sessions continued, often my clients would ask "how long will I need to continue with therapy?" My response was, "When I hand you the mirror and you say 'thank you,' you're ready to go!"

Write the affirmation and response:

This process helps you identify the reasons a part of you is telling you why you can't have what you want. Take a piece of paper and make two columns. In the first one, write your affirmation. In the second column, write the immediate response that pops into your mind. Write the affirmation again, and then the response. Usually, as you write the affirmation over and over, the negative responses shift into positive ones. You are reinforcing the new belief, and your subconscious is accepting the new belief. There are two examples on the next page. Read them, and then practice with your own examples.

Try an affirmation bath:

At the workshops I lead, we often do a process called an affirmation bath. Participants form groups of five, so that one person can sit in the center and receive the "bath" from the other four people. Here's how it works: write out about ten affirmations about yourself and your life that you really want to manifest. Include ones that counteract any negative ideas

Affirmation	Response
I am in a wonderful relationship.	You? You don't deserve it!
I am in a wonderful relationship.	You aren't attractive enough.
I AM in a wonderful relationship.	It's possible.
I AM in a wonderful relationship.	Maybe.
I AM in a wonderful relationship.	Yes, it feels great.
I always have enough money to pay my bills ahead of time.	No way.
I always have enough money to pay my bills ahead of time.	With what?
I always have enough money to pay my bills ahead of time.	Hard to believe.
I <u>always</u> have enough money to pay my bills ahead of time.	Maybe sometimes.
I <u>always</u> have enough money to pay my bills ahead of time.	I'm willing to believe.
I ALWAYS have enough money to pay my bills ahead of time.	Yes, I accept prosperity.

you were given in childhood about yourself. Make four copies to give to the others in your group to read to you when you're in the center. Each person has about five minutes to sit in the center and receive their affirmation bath. The other four continually read the affirmations in different orders (so everyone isn't saying the same affirmation at the same time). It sounds somewhat chaotic, but the result is that the conscious mind isn't fast enough to block all four voices, and the affirmations really begin to "sink in" at the emotional level.

Talk to your Inner Child:

Close your eyes and imagine yourself as a child of five or six. How does the child feel? What does the child need? What comforting and encouraging words from you does the child need to hear? Your consciousness carries all the positive and negative memories from your childhood. There isn't really one "inner child." There are numerous experiences that shaped your ideas about yourself and all of life from every age that are still a part of your conscious and unconscious minds. The inner child exercise and the others listed above are designed to help you remember more of the unconscious beliefs that are limiting you. In–residence workshops are often an excellent way to do healing work with the inner child.

Using these techniques will assist you in developing awareness of the limiting beliefs you have been using to send orders to the Cosmic Kitchen. With this new awareness, you can begin to send in the new orders. Some people feel guilty when they start to create a wonderful new life for themselves. Somehow it seems to be a betrayal to their parents and others they grew up with, or they feel selfish. If you are having some of those feelings.....

GET OVER THEM!

In the United States, there is a poster for recruiting for the Army, and it says Uncle Sam needs YOU. Well.....

THE UNIVERSE NEEDS <u>YOU</u>!

That's right, the Universe needs you and your energy to help everyone shift. The more you open up to joy and happiness, the more you help others. *A Course in Miracles*, a spiritual course I've studied for years, says that for every five minutes you spend in the light, a thousand minds open to a new way of seeing. That is an amazing idea. You're doing this work, not just for yourself, but for the entire planet. Now, this doesn't mean your mother will suddenly go along with these ideas. But at a collective conscious level, your changes help everyone.

On the next page are some affirmations to reinforce clearing the old menu and welcoming a wonderful new life. On the last page of the chapter, write your own Cosmic Kitchen orders by looking at the list of negative beliefs you wrote at the beginning of this chapter and changing them into the positive orders you are now creating.

Affirmations to clear old menu items:

I choose to believe that it is easy to clear the menu items I no longer want.

I am willing to open my arms and claim the wonderful life I deserve.

Any resource I need for my emotional and spiritual healing comes to me quickly and easily, whether it is a book, tape, or practitioner.

I have clear insights that assist me in releasing the past.

I do believe that I deserve a fun and exciting life.

I greet the morning with joy and enthusiasm.

I begin my new life in this moment.

I do love myself. Yes I do, yes I do!

My positive shifts help everyone.

Orders for My New Menu.....

I easily set aside a special time each day to practice meditation and visualization. My mind, body, and spirit are nurtured and energized by the experience. I rejoice in creating the new "inner landscapes" that produce change on the outside.

Chapter 4

Meditation and Visualization

Meditation and visualization are two powerful techniques that will help you focus energy on your orders and speed up the Cosmic Kitchen. Being a girl from a conservative family in New Jersey, I never expected to be advocating meditation, but here's how it happened:

I'll always remember the first time I flew into Los Angeles airport. As we were descending, I saw this awful layer of brown, and I said to the man sitting next to me, "what's that?" He looked at me as though I were quite dense, and said "that's smog!" Smog—

ick—how ugly. I had no idea the sky in LA would look like this. I thought California was sunny and beautiful. What about all those Beach Boys songs?

I had never been to LA before, but here I was on my way to start a master's program in chemistry (it's a long story) at the University of Southern California. During my junior year at a college near Chicago, I had decided that I wanted to apply to graduate school "someplace warm." Without ever visiting there, I settled on California and applied to two schools, USC and UCLA. UCLA turned me down completely, but USC gave me a teaching fellowship, so there wasn't even a choice. As the plane descended, I had no idea that my outer journey to California would trigger an inner journey and spiritual quest. But as my mom grew to be fond of saying, "You people in California are about ten years ahead of us folks on the east coast." At the time, I hadn't recognized my inner longing as a search for my spiritual connection. I thought it was only a longing to be in a new place.

About three weeks into the semester at USC, I knew the chemistry program wasn't for me. My courses in college simply hadn't prepared me. Fortunately, my teaching position was for a very basic course, so that went well. And I discovered that I loved teaching, something I would return to years later. But <u>now</u> I needed a job. It appeared in the form of a social worker position in Watts. The stress of the job led me to meditation.

Eastern meditation masters often refer to the human mind as the "monkey mind" because it seems to jump all over the place. Before starting to meditate, it did seem that my mind raced in many different directions and I had difficulty focusing and concentrating on anything for very long.

When I began meditating in the early seventies, even in California it was considered strange and weird. At that time many of my friends thought that smoking a joint was the answer to stress. Celebrities like the Beatles and Mia Farrow were starting to meditate, though, so it gained some popularity. Meditation changed my life so dramatically for the better, I would preach about the benefits to anyone who would listen. I'm sure I was rather obnoxious at times, but I wanted everyone to feel as wonderful as I did.

Meditation is a simple process of focusing your attention on the breath or on a short phrase called a mantra. This process will take you to a quiet and relaxed state. This allows you to balance emotionally, physically, mentally and spiritually. If there were a pill that did that, it would be the most popular one available! When you're in that quiet place, your heart and mind are connected, so doing your affirmations at this level is even more powerful than simply repeating them when you are in your usual conscious state. My own journey with meditation began as a stress reduction method, but it evolved into a spiritual practice as I experienced the heart–mind connection and a feeling of being connected to "something" greater than myself. It is clear to me that many of the manifestations I created in my life before even knowing about affirmations were a result of my daily meditation practice.

If you're already meditating regularly, terrific. Keep it up. If not, are you ready to change your life for the better? There are many books on meditation and many groups you can attend to learn and practice meditation, so I'll just give you a few basic techniques here.

Sit comfortably. Loosen any restrictive cloth-ing. Gently close your eyes. Breathe deeply and easily. Focus your attention on your breathing. As you breathe in, think to your-self, "I am...." and as you breathe out, think to yourself, "relaxed." Do this several times. Let your shoulders, jaw, and back relax and let go. Then, beginning at the top of your head, move your consciousness slowly down through your body scanning for tension. Any place that you feel tension, pause and imagine breath-ing in relaxation to that part of your body and breathing out the tension. Continue this process until your entire body feels relaxed. FEEL yourself becoming more and more re-laxed, peaceful, and happy. Return to the thought, "I am...." as you breathe in and "re-laxed" as you breathe out. Stay with this thought for ten to twenty minutes. Then slowly bring your attention back to the moment. Be-

*come aware of the room and the chair or sofa
you are sitting on. Breathe more deeply.
Stretch, begin to move your arms and legs,
and then slowly open your eyes. Take a few
minutes to return to your usual activity level.*

There are numerous other methods for achieving
a deeply relaxed state. You might want to try different ones to find the one that helps you the most. Here
are some suggestions:

❖ Count your breaths from one to four. Simply
count mentally each time you exhale, starting with
one and going to four. Repeat the counting over
and over.

❖ Think to yourself, "calm and serene" with each
breath, or any other phrase that is relaxing for
you.

❖ Visualize yourself in a beautiful, peaceful set-
ting. Once you are relaxed, gently think your
affirmations.

When you practice meditation, do so before eating a meal, or wait a half–hour after eating a light
meal and at least an hour after eating a large one.
Take the phone off the hook and recognize that this
is a special time for nurturing yourself. You may find
that playing soothing music in the background helps
you achieve greater relaxation. Some people prefer
using guided meditation to help them relax. There

are many tapes available. Ones that I've recorded are listed at the end of the book. You can also tape any of the previous instructions for yourself.

Practicing meditation and gaining the many benefits from it does take time and commitment. Start where you can with the time you have and you will soon be motivated to take at least fifteen minutes a day for this wonderful self–nurturing and rejuvenating technique. Your experience with meditation will differ from day to day. I've enjoyed many moments of great bliss in meditation, feeling as though I was in a timeless place, and also many moments of having difficulty focusing. The important thing is to JUST DO IT, just like the Nike commercials say, and the results will speak for themselves. Now on to visualization.

Visualizations are imagining, seeing, feeling, or describing something you would like to create. They bring in all of the senses along with affirmations to give your subconscious mind the EXPERIENCE of the reality you are creating. Your subconscious mind doesn't know the difference between the reality "out there" and the one you create inside, so visualizations create a new "inner landscape" that in turn produces results on the outside. Many people say they cannot visualize, yet they can always describe their backyard or kitchen. That is a form of visualization. When we can somehow picture or feel what it is we want, then we're visualizing. It's really that simple. The feeling part is actually more important than really "seeing" the new reality, as the Universe responds most quickly to the feelings you send out.

Visualization can be used to imagine a new career, greater prosperity, a wonderful relationship, vibrant health, traveling to exotic destinations, changing habits, and connecting with your Inner Wisdom. Indeed, the uses of this technique are endless. It can also be used to neutralize the past. You can imagine speaking to the "inner child" part of you that was taught to believe in limitations and tell her or him about the new reality of abundance you are creating.

In her book *Creative Visualization*, Shakti Gawain identifies four steps for visualization. First, decide exactly what it is you want to create. Second, create the mental picture or a feeling of what you are creating. Include as many details as possible. Use powerful images that embody what you are creating, such as an image of the ocean as your source of abundance. Third, focus lightly on this picture or feeling during meditation times as well as during the day. Finally, use positive affirmations to give your goal additional positive energy.

On the next page, there is a sample visualization for increased prosperity. Read it slowly, then close your eyes and go through it mentally, really feeling as though this has already happened in your life.

On the last page of the chapter, take a few minutes to write down a brief visualization for something <u>you</u> want to create.

Visualization for Prosperity

Take a deep breath. Allow your body to relax.....
Take several slow easy breaths.....

Now imagine yourself in a beautiful meadow. Look around at the green grass stretching across the meadow and the array of brightly colored wildflowers. You become aware of the abundance of nature. You can really feel it. This abundance of nature is yours as well. Really feel it! Now imagine yourself at the beach. The fine sand stretches out all around you and the ocean shimmers in front of you. If you began counting the grains of sand, you would never finish. If you began dipping a large bowl in the ocean, there would always be more. This is like the prosperity of the Universe. It is limitless!

Now bring to mind something you want to manifest.... It could be increased money, a special vacation, a car, whatever you want. Right now, imagine that it has already happened and is a reality in your life. Use all your senses in imagining the reality of it. Really feel it as strongly as you can. Stay with the images and feelings for a few minutes. Then take some deep, easy breaths and bring your awareness back to the room where you're sitting. Become aware of your surroundings, stretch, and slowly open your eyes.

My Visualization....

In this moment, I choose to believe that the Universe is abundant and that I am deserving of all good. I am a part of the Universal flow of energy in an ocean of abundance. Every day I express gratitude for all that is a part of my life.

Chapter 5

Money and Material Orders

There is enough money on this planet for everyone (yes, everyone) to have a million dollars! So you may be wondering why Bill Gates has BILLIONS and some people have a million, and you don't know where the next hundred is coming from. The answer is simple: consciousness. Each of us has played out the beliefs from childhood about deservability and money to create whatever we have in our lives right at this moment. Now, don't start any of that blame or guilt stuff. You can begin to change your consciousness about money and material things RIGHT NOW.

When leading prosperity workshops, I tell the group that the answer to financial well–being is <u>not</u> more money. There is usually a short stunned silence after I say that. Then I go on to explain that if we redistributed all the billions on the planet tomorrow and no one changed their consciousness about money, it would all be back to the same people in the same amounts in about six months. The answer is changing your beliefs about what you deserve to receive.

What did you learn about money and material things growing up? Do you remember your parents arguing about how to spend money? Take a few minutes to sit quietly. Close your eyes and allow your mind to gently drift back in time to some significant experience about money when you were growing up. What happened? What was the belief you developed from that experience? If it was limiting, imagine yourself as that child and begin to tell the child that it's time to create a new set of ideas about money that are expansive and supportive. Tell the child what those new affirmations are. If the experience you remembered helped you with positive thoughts about money, reinforce those with your inner child.

Ask yourself: who would you betray if you were financially successful? When I ask that question in my courses, the answer is often mom or dad (or both.) Somehow, the child part feels that to go beyond the parents' limitations is not OK. You can close your eyes and talk to mom or dad, or anyone else who had a significant influence on your prosperity beliefs, and tell them that it's OK for both of you to be prosperous and successful. Go to the mirror and do the same thing. Be willing to go past old limitations.

An incident that happened to me many years ago demonstrated how I had unconsciously limited myself. During my college years, my mother would take me shopping for clothes at the end of the summer. Just before my senior year we went shopping as usual. I needed a new coat, and it had to be a warm one because my college was near Chicago, Illinois, and the winters were really cold. On this particular shopping day, I saw the most beautiful coat I had ever seen. It was camel colored, long, warm and fit perfectly. And it was on sale. But even on sale it was more than Mom would have normally spent for me on clothes, and we still had more shopping to do. She looked at my face and saw how much I wanted that coat, smiled, and took it to the counter to pay for it. I was so excited. This stunning coat was perfect.

A week later I was on a flight from Newark, New Jersey to the Chicago airport. There was so much to pack I carried my raincoat and my beautiful new coat. Once in Chicago, two friends and I hailed a cab to take us to the college housing. With three of us, we were tightly packed in the back of the cab, and so my coats went up behind the seat. When we arrived at the college, we all piled out and started taking our suitcases upstairs. About fifteen minutes later, I suddenly realized that I had left my coats in the cab! Feeling panicked, I couldn't even remember the name of the cab company, and neither could my friends. I started calling companies in the phone book, asking if any of their cabbies had reported the forgotten coats. No, no, no. I felt devastated. How would I tell Mom the expensive coat was lost? Why had I been so dumb as to lose it? It was many years before I understood why I had unconsciously forgotten the coat. It was because my belief was, "you can have nice things, but not what you REALLY want because it's too expensive." The coat had been what I really wanted, and that was opposite my belief, so I lost it before I even wore it. When I realized that, I could stop blaming myself for the loss. My new affirmation became "I deserve to receive exactly what I want and I have the money to pay for it."

As you go about your daily routine for the next few days, be aware of your thoughts about money and material things. Do you tell yourself you can't have things? Pay attention to your thoughts when you go to spend money. Notice what you think about people that seem to have a lot of money and people that seem to have little money. When you become aware of thoughts that are limiting, create an affirmation for the new belief you want to send to the Cosmic Kitchen.

CAUTION: Affirmations are not intended to be an excuse so that you can spend money irresponsibly. Running up large credit card bills while affirming that the Universe will take care of them is not good money management. There are three parts to money matters: mental/emotional matters, practical matters, and spiritual matters. First, you need to identify the old beliefs and emotions about money that no longer serve you. Then you want to create affirmations for the new beliefs. Next, you need to be honest with yourself about the practical matters. Are you balancing your checkbook? Are you able to pay off your credit cards each month? If not, do you have a plan to be debt–free? Create a plan to handle the practical money matters. Third, you must recognize that the Universe is your Source, not a job and not a person. John Randolph Price's book, *The Abundance Book*, is excellent for training your consciousness to the abundance of Spirit.

It does take faith and trust to believe that you deserve prosperity when you're looking at your checkbook and there is $100 in your account and the rent that is due is $500. A few months after purchasing my condominium, I was sitting in the laundromat waiting for my clothes to dry, and decided to balance my checkbook and estimate my income and expenses for the month. Within a few minutes, it was clear I didn't have enough money to pay my mortgage, much less any other bills. At the time, as a psychologist intern, my income depended on the number of clients I saw each week. It was after the Christmas holidays, and traditionally people don't seek therapy in January. I had no savings to use.

Even though I had been practicing the techniques in this book for years, in that moment I felt devastated. I sat in the laundromat and started to cry, wondering why the Universe had allowed me to purchase my first home if I would have to give it up so soon. (These thoughts were rather extreme, but perhaps you can relate.) I went home, put away my clothes, and headed straight for the small loft in my condo. This was my meditation room. I sank down on the floor, and began to breathe deeply to relax, and then spent over an hour in meditation, connecting with Spirit as my Source, and saying my affirmations after I felt more peaceful. They were: "I am safe. All the money I need for my mortgage and other expenses is provided for me. I express my gratitude to the Universe for all its abundance."

The next day I did the same thing, and the next. I cultivated that place of perfect trust. But I also asked myself, "What is the worst that could happen?" Well, the worst would be that I'd have to sell the condo and not have a place to live. Could I handle that? It wouldn't be my choice, but I could. Could I find another place? Of course. In fact, it even occurred to me that I could leave southern California completely and go to Esalen (a fantastic conference and retreat center in northern California) and do work study there. There *were* options, regardless of what happened with my condo. And then the phone started to ring. Within a week, I had fourteen new clients scheduled. Not only did I have enough to pay my mortgage, there was enough to pay other bills and buy groceries. This was a powerful example of trusting!

Perhaps the following story will also help you develop trust.

Delia is an enthusiastic and passionate woman from Liverpool, England, who knows that ordering from the Cosmic Kitchen works. A few years ago she was working part–time as a registered "childminder" (a very English term), picking up children after school, and then watching them until time to take them home. However, she'd always been a frustrated artist, and decided to make an investment in herself by taking a "Paint Effects Course." Afterwards, she spent a few hundred pounds on advertising for her painting, planning to continue the childminding until the painting business got going. But in her mind she had really decided to "go for" the painting, and the next thing she knew, her childcare was terminated, and no painting jobs had started yet.

The last day of her childcare contract, Delia took the children to a funhouse. As they played she sat with pen, paper, and bank statement. When the credits and debits were recorded, she saw with dismay that she was very much "in the red," with no apparent prospects for income. There were a few minutes of desperation and misery, and then she remembered: I know how to do affirmations. Inside, a light had switched on. She tore up the credits and debits statement and wrote and wrote:

"MY TALENTS ARE RECOGNIZED. MY TALENTS ARE IN DEMAND. I OPEN MY ARMS TO PROSPERITY."

57

Driving home, the children giggled as she repeated the affirmations out loud. She felt inspired and excited. After dropping off the children, Delia drove home, still saying her affirmations. As she pulled up to her home, she heard the phone ringing. Rushing inside she answered it. The caller was Lorraine, a previous customer. Lorraine said she had been telling a woman writer for the Liverpool Echo about Delia and her work, and they wanted to do a feature. Was she interested? Within a week, Delia's photo and a full page article entitled "The Woman Who Turned Her Hobby into a Business" about her and her work appeared in the newspaper. The phone began ringing off the hook with inquiries and her business took off. Now, if the phone is quiet, her husband will say, "Open your arms and do that affirmation stuff!"

The Cosmic Kitchen has a talent for fulfilling orders in a manner different from your expectations. For a number of years I have been leading weekend courses and workshops. I learned a wonderful lesson in trust when organizing my very first one. It was to be held at a beautiful health retreat in California called Murrieta Hot Springs Resort. I told my clients and advertised it. However, as the deposit deadline approached there were only a few people signed up. The deposit to the resort was due, and because of my lack of experience I hadn't set the deposit amount high enough to pay them the amount they required to reserve the rooms. And there wasn't anything extra in my account. So, all week I affirmed for six deposit checks. On Friday, I went to my P.O. box and peeked in. Only one envelope. How was I going to pay the resort? With a sinking feeling, I reached in and pulled out the one envelope and opened it. Inside was a check for the FULL amount of the weekend for a husband and wife who were registering and that amount was <u>exactly</u> what six deposits would have been. Once again, I was grateful to the Universe for finding the best way to fulfill my order, one I had not thought of.

Like many people, Diane had been raised to believe that money didn't grow on trees and that you had to work hard and be frugal. Diane attended one of my training programs in England. As part of the training, each person leads a forty–five minute session in a small group toward the end of the week. Diane decided that she would give hers on prosperity, since this was something she wanted to learn. As she prepared for the presentation, this beautiful visualization came to her:

Close your eyes and start to breathe deeply. Begin to relax. Remember you are safe and divinely guided. Take deep breaths, relax your shoulders and visualize the brightest star in the galaxy. It shines so brilliantly among all the other hundreds of stars and is becoming brighter and brighter. This moment is sus-

pended in time. It is a moment of anticipation, of wonder, of infinite possibility.

Suddenly, the star—your star—shoots though the galaxy, gathering power and energy as it courses its way towards you. Its powerful ray enters through the top of your head. You have never felt such power, such magnetism, such peace. You are one with the God who made you. You are one with all the stars in the galaxy; the abundance of the Universe is yours. Feel yourself become a Divine magnet for all the prosperity you deserve!

The power of this beautiful star travels down through your body until it passes out through your toes and you are as one continuous stream of light connecting you to the nurturing planet earth and the galaxy of stars. You are now drawing all the prosperity and abundance of the Universe to you. Feel the peace as your dreams of health, wealth, loving relationships, and success in your career are realized. Take as long as you like to really experience these wonderful feelings. Bring these feelings to you every time you say your positive affirmation, "I am divinely abundant and a magnet for success." Then release your dreams with gratitude to the Universe to manifest for you on the earthly plane.

After her presentation, Diane was exhilarated by

the experience and ran to the telephone to call her husband. Excitedly, she told him about deciding to present on prosperity, and how well it had gone. There was a short silence, and then he told her, "Perhaps that explains why you received a check today for your raise!" Diane gasped— she had been negotiating for months for the raise without success, and it arrived today, of all possible days.

Are you ready to let go of your limiting beliefs about prosperity and welcome your abundance? On the next page there are a number of prosperity affirmations. Read them, sing them, open your arms and be willing to believe them. Then write some of your own. Know that you DESERVE the abundance of the Universe.

Affirmations for prosperity:

I am a money magnet!
Unexpected income is always coming my way.

❖

Every day my relationship with money
becomes healthier.

❖

My income is constantly increasing as my
expenses stay proportionately the same or less!

❖

All of my needs are met by the
Universal abundance of Spirit.

❖

I always have enough money to pay
my bills ahead of time.

❖

I choose to embrace thoughts of abundance
that nurture and support me.

❖

I am confident that I earn a wonderful living
doing work and service that is important to me.

❖

I welcome an abundance of joy, love,
and money into my life.

❖

I believe that money is my friend and I
deserve to receive it in abundance.

My Prosperity Orders....

It is wonderful to be using my unique skills and abilities doing work and service that is important to me. It is delightful to be working with other creative and like-minded people. I welcome abundant financial compensation for my work.

Chapter 6

Career and Success Orders

Before even understanding the concepts of affirmations and the Cosmic Kitchen, I manifested a number of jobs: social worker, rehabilitation worker, teaching assistant, and community college teacher. Once I understood how this had happened, I consciously began to use these concepts to continue creating new career opportunities for myself. And so can you!

In 1981, my job was administering worksite wellness programs under a state grant. This was a position I had affirmed for and gotten, but once in the job

I realized that administration wasn't my cup of tea. I wanted to be <u>teaching</u> the courses in stress management and other wellness topics, not organizing others to do them. While the job had some exciting aspects, my real joy was in sharing information that helped people live their lives in healthier, happier ways. So I began affirming, "I have a wonderful job teaching, making the same or greater salary that I have now. I have time to work on my doctoral dissertation and I am also able to complete my contract here." I would occasionally think or say the affirmations.

A few months went by. One day, the phone rang in my office. The person on the other end of the line identified himself as Ken Ravizza, a professor at California State University–Fullerton. He had gotten my name from a mutual acquaintance who said I was "into holistic health." He told me he was going on sabbatical next year and needed someone to teach his stress management course. He asked me to come to his class the next month and give a lecture that he could tape and then give to the department head. Of course I said yes, and the date was set. I spoke to his class on using communication skills to reduce stress. It took several months before it was confirmed that I was hired for the next year. I was able to finish my contract with the state, have a few months in the summer to work on my dissertation, and then do want I love: teach. Working with the students was wonderful, and I so enjoyed complementing their strictly academic classes with practical techniques for living life more fully. The class became so popular that even after Ken returned from sabbatical I was able to continue teaching the course. For eight years I taught stress management at the university, until my private practice became so busy there was no time for both.

After completing my Ph.D., I kept teaching part–time and decided to take a few months to decide what else I wanted to do. Occasionally I would get calls from people who wanted to know if I did individual work. I always said "no" and referred them to someone else. Then one day the lightbulb went on. The Universe was sending me clients and I was turning them away. Although my degree was in social psychology, I had quite a bit of counseling background, and always loved working with people. So, the next person who called, I said "Yes, I do individual work." Since I didn't have an office, the person came to my home. Soon I had several clients.

However, there were some drawbacks to working at home. The living room was the counseling room, so my husband had to be banished to the bedroom if I had an evening client. Plus, I guided clients through a lot of meditation and visualization, and our dogs always sensed the energy and started barking right by the living room window. It became clear I needed an office. But where? I started affirming for the perfect office space. I looked at a few ads in the paper and the rents seemed high even for poor locations. One day I decided to do a breath session to gain clarity about the situation. For forty–five minutes I did intense connected breathing, and didn't get one insight. But when I was done, without thinking, I went to the kitchen, opened the daily newspaper to the classified section, and there—to my delight—was a little ad that said: "Share holistic health office." Quickly, I called the number and spoke to Rhonda. She had a reflexology/acupressure practice and sounded wonderful on the phone. Then she told me the price of the office. $400, just for one room! In 1986, this seemed like a lot of money to spend monthly on an office. But for some reason I made an appointment to see it. As I drove over there the next day, my negative self-talk kicked in: *why are you going to see this office? You know you can't afford it. This is a waste of time. Blah, blah, blah.*

When I arrived, Rhonda was still with a client, so I just looked around. The office was in a great location, on Pacific Coast Highway in Seal Beach. Inside, there was a soothing plush deep green carpet and comfortable furniture in the waiting room. And then I saw the prayer that I said every day from *A Course in Miracles*, right by the door of the room available for rent. It seemed like a sign. I'm sure you can guess that I moved to that office within a few weeks.

It was an exciting time. The office was only fifteen minutes from my home, I gave weekly mini-workshops, and my client base was increasing. Then one day Rhonda asked me out to lunch. I thought, *how nice, this is the first time we've been out to lunch.* But the news she told me completely took away my appetite. She had bought a condo in Huntington Beach and had found an office to rent with a physician there. Unless I wanted to take over the rent of $1,000 a month in Seal Beach, I would need to find another office, too. I was crushed. The current one was so perfect. What I didn't realize at the time was that some other Cosmic Orders I had been putting out were getting fulfilled.

Rhonda was moving to an office in a lovely and very unusual shopping area called Seacliff Village. There were beautiful ceramic murals with seascapes, and special displays about birds outside around the complex. It had a wonderful feel to it, and also happened to be the location for the church I was attending. A few days after our lunch, Rhonda told me that the physician had one other office to rent out, if I was interested. The rent was less than $200 (the good news) but at least a half hour from my home (the bad news.) Then I remembered thinking many times in the past, "The energy is so wonderful in Seacliff Village. I'd love to work there." Although I did find the drive tedious at times, the office move to Seacliff Village turned out to be a pivotal time for me, as I began taking classes at the church that deepened my understanding of the Universe and how it works. And within a few months, my desire to be of greater service was fulfilled when a gay man who knew I had studied with Louise Hay asked me to lead an AIDS support group at the church. For over two years I led that group every Monday night. It was one of my most powerful learning experiences.

The Universe seems to enjoy fulfilling orders in a way that is different from what you expect. Elizabeth

69

is a tall, beautiful brunette. From years of a spiritual practice, her inner beauty truly shines as well. When I first met her at one of my training sessions, I thought she must have been a model. Later I discovered that she had been a dancer, working at the MGM Grand in Reno and other places. Years later, she was working as a talent agent in Las Vegas, but not enjoying it very much, when she heard that MGM was opening a new hotel in Vegas. Elizabeth felt really excited about working there behind the scenes in the entertainment area. It would be like "going home," since she had previously worked at MGM and loved their movies growing up. After five hours of applications and interviews (all the while knowing she would be the perfect employee) she never heard anything. Elizabeth was so disappointed. Why didn't she get a job there? Others she knew had. It certainly didn't seem fair.

Despite her disappointment, Elizabeth continued doing her affirmations. As she power–walked in the mornings, she said affirmations to the rhythm of her walk, "I work in a job that I love. My perfect job comes to me. I make good money. I am at peace with the flow of life."

Within a short period of time, "out of the blue" she received a call from Leslie, an ex–dancer who worked at the MGM theme park. They hadn't spoken in years. Would Elizabeth like to work with her, supervising the entertainers at the theme park? Of course! She asked Leslie if she had seen her résumé and application, and that's why she had decided to call. No—the idea had just come to Leslie that she'd like to work with Elizabeth.

This part–time position was the perfect job. Within a year she was promoted to create a convention entertainment plan for the theme park. She worked there several years, and was given more and more responsibility because she did such an excellent job. Eventually, it was time to move on. She was being called to a different type of work which allows her to express her spiritual values and a message of personal growth and development. Elizabeth now works with individuals and teaches transformational workshops using the principles in this book.

If you are a morning person, and enjoy inspiration, hearing a good speaker, a supportive community of people dedicated to personal and planetary transformation, and lots of hugging, you would love the Inside Edge. It's a breakfast meeting from 6:30–8:30 A.M. every Wednesday in Orange County, Calif. Started by Diana von Welanetz Wentworth and her late husband Paul in 1986, this group has been a continuing source of inspiration for me. (And now you can experience it without flying to California– check out the live Internet broadcast at www.insideedge.org.)

One particular morning, the room was filled with laughter. The speaker was Barbara Sher, author of *Wishcraft*. Barbara has a knack for finding humor in the simplest of situations. This morning her topic was achieving our dreams. Partway through her talk, she asked each person to get a partner and tell that person

71

our dream. In my mind I planned to say, "I am a nationally known workshop leader." Instead, what popped out of my mouth was "I am an internationally known workshop leader!" I was stunned—where did that affirmation come from? Little did I know then that within a few years I would be traveling and leading workshops internationally. As I look back, it's amazing how the Cosmic Kitchen arranged everything.

In 1986, I had met Louise Hay at this same breakfast group, signed up for her mailing list, and later attended two week–long intensives that she led. After that, she asked me to be a small group leader at subsequent intensives, plus giving a presentation. Then in late 1988, too busy to do them all herself, she asked four of us who had taught in the intensives to start leading her weekend workshop, *Love Yourself, Heal Your Life*. Over the next few years, I led the workshop in the United States and Canada, so my affirmation to be an "international workshop leader" had been fulfilled. Little did I know at that time that much more was to come. A British woman from Birmingham, England named Norma Jarvis began affirming to put Birmingham on the map metaphysically. The Cosmic Coordinator went to work to bring us together.

Norma wrote to Hay House asking Louise to come to Birmingham, and was instead referred to me. When Norma contacted me, I was delighted. I had spent the summer of '67 in England and loved it. It seemed like my "second home," so I was excited about returning. The weekend workshops in England were wonderfully successful, and led to my also leading them in Spain, Italy, Poland, and Greece (all with interpreters—now that's a unique experience.) After a few years the students in England asked me to create a training program to allow them to share this life–changing work. The training workshops were led in England, San Diego, and Australia, training hundreds of workshop leaders. I could never have imagined all of the events that led to the fulfillment of my order to be an internationally known workshop leader. However, my greatest satisfaction was receiving cards, calls, and emails from those I had trained, sharing with me how life–changing the work was for their students. Miracles of healing occurred every time a workshop was held. The desire I had held in my heart since childhood, to be a part of healing the planet, had happened, without my knowing how it would happen.

What are YOUR dreams and desires for your career? What are your unique skills and abilities? If you already know specifically what you want to do as a career, create some powerful affirmations for that career. If you're not sure, affirm that you have clarity about your career path.

On the next page are some affirmations about deserving and creating your ideal livelihood. Following that is a blank page for your specific affirmations. Go for it. Be outrageous! The Cosmic Kitchen waits with all the ingredients to fulfill your order.

Affirmations for career:

*I am using my unique skills and abilities
to work in my perfect career.*

I now have clarity about my career path.

*I am confident that I earn a wonderful living doing
work and service that is important to me.*

*The Cosmic Chef arranges for me to meet those who
will assist me in my career.*

*It's so exciting to be earning a good living using my
special talents.*

*It is delightful to be working with creative, loving,
supportive people.*

My Career Orders.....

Chapter 7

Healthy Orders

When you were growing up, how did your parents talk about health and illness? Do you remember hearing, "I always get a cold after Christmas" or "When the flu is going around, I always catch it?" What diseases were you told "run in the family?" Most of us were brought up to believe that we had no responsibility for the health and well–being of our bodies. It was as though some "other mind" was in charge of what happened in them. Those ideas are gradually changing as more and more people (including doctors) become aware that the mind and body are a system, not separate entities with no communication.

In late 2000, my life partner Rick and I started a series of telecourses, courses that were held by telephone using a conference call line. Using the telephone has allowed us to reach people all over the USA and other countries with metaphysical courses. During our *Abundant Life* series, one session was about the body/mind connection. As we talked about affirmations, one woman mentioned that she was "always tired." There was no physical dis–ease that she was aware of, but she often felt tired and told herself, "I'm tired." I gave her one of my favorite affirmations, "I sleep in peace and wake in joy" and Rick suggested she also say to herself "I feel great in the morning" as she was falling asleep and "I feel great" when she awoke. The next week we started our telephone course as usual. Lida could barely contain herself. "I feel great!" she exclaimed. She was excited to have experienced an improvement so quickly. (Please note: I am not suggesting that you ignore feelings of fatigue or dis–ease in your body. Listening to your body intuitively and paying attention to its signals are very important. However, in this case, Lida had simply been reinforcing a thought that she was "tired" for so long that it kept manifesting. Changing the thought changed her experience quite dramatically in a very short period of time.)

For the next few days, notice how you think and talk about your body and your physical energy. Which thoughts are serving you and which ones are not? At the end of this chapter, write down the orders about your body that you want to place in the Cosmic Kitchen.

Our bodies not only listen and respond to our words and feelings, they store feelings that aren't resolved. Cynthia, a lovely woman from England, discovered that by changing her words and dealing with her old anger she could heal a bladder infection that had plagued her for several years and had failed to respond to repeated treatment with antibiotics. After taking one of my courses, Cynthia began to notice that she used the phrase "I am pissed off" a lot. She eliminated those words from her vocabulary, and then began using alternative treatments and dealing with her emotional self. She was able to remember and release anxiety, fear, and anger from her childhood experiences and then forgive. The bladder infections healed completely. Her order to the Cosmic Kitchen was fulfilled, but it also took a period of time because she had to deal with the emotions that had been stored in her body. When you are dealing with a chronic condition or a life threatening illness, working with a skilled therapist who can guide you through the release process is a good idea.

A wonderful affirmation to use when you're going through a healing process is: "Every resource I need for my healing, whether a health professional, alternative treatment, book, tape, or anything else, comes to me quickly and easily." Trust that you will be guided to the perfect resource for you at the perfect time.

All my life I had been energetic and involved with many activities and projects. However, after working as a psychological intern for a few years, I began to notice that I seemed to need an extra meditation in the afternoon to feel alert enough to see my clients in the evening. My hours of sleep increased and I wasn't interested in going out on the weekends. Although affirming for vibrant energy, that didn't seem to be happening. When I finally went to my acupuncturist, he gave me a diagnosis of chronic fatigue syndrome.

Immediately I began to read about CFS. I made changes in my diet, eliminating sugar and processed foods (I had already cut out caffeine and alcohol.) Natural herbal supplements strengthened my immune system along with regular acupuncture appointments, and I regularly gave myself Reiki treatments (Reiki is a hands–on healing technique.) But most important, I discovered how vital it was to focus my energy on significant projects, rather than spreading it out in many different directions. A psychic once told me, "Patricia, you have two speeds: 250 miles an hour or zero." Now it was time to learn to go a reasonable speed. As my healing progressed and my usual high energy level returned, I noticed that if I went into my old pattern of "too many projects" the fatigue would return. In addition, the realization struck that I couldn't always just sit home and meditate to achieve healing, but also needed the help of some professionals. It was an amazing learning process.

A wonderful book for gleaning some insight into the mental/emotional patterns that are a part of dis–ease is called *Heal Your Body* by Louise Hay. It provides a starting point for healing by identifying some common patterns and offering helpful affirmations to change the patterns. For myself and my clients, this book has been about 85% accurate in identifying the probable causes of a particular symptom or dis–ease. In addition to the affirmations, however, treatments with physicians or alternative practitioners, or deep emotional work may be necessary for healing. The healing path for each person is different, so you must pay attention to inner guidance to find yours.

It's OK to be bold in your affirmations for health and healing. Tell the Universe, "I claim a healing NOW." Visualize yourself healthy and well. Hold the feeling of wellness in your consciousness as strongly as possible. In meditation, ask "what do I need to know for my complete healing?" At the end of this book there is a list of my favorite books for promoting healing on all levels. Let your intuition guide you in choosing one or more to read.

One spring in California I developed a severe allergy, with lots of sneezing and congestion. Giving myself Reiki treatments plus using affirmations and meditation didn't seem to help. The "probable causes" in Louise's book didn't fit. Finally, during a special intuitive meditation, I received the message to go to a traditional physician for diagnosis and treatment. What? I had medical insurance, but hadn't been to a traditional physician in years. After several days of continued misery with the allergy and wondering why I couldn't just heal it myself, I received a message in meditation to go to a certain urgent care clinic near my home, with the information there would be a young male doctor who was open to alternative work who would be very helpful.

The next day, at the clinic, I saw a young male doctor. He was understanding about the alternative work, but he also gave me a prescription that cleared the allergy in only a few days. With that experience, I realized how important it was to recognize that Spirit has given us a RANGE of resources for healing: traditional and alternative practitioners, healthy foods and vitamins, as well as our own minds and emotional selves.

True healing is a process of mind, body, and spirit. All three elements must be addressed. If you are a person who tends to go to a medical doctor or alternative practitioner frequently, but you are not taking responsibility for yourself by eating well, meditating, and exploring possible emotional connections to your disease, it is important for you to address these aspects as well. If, like me, you have a tendency to want to "do it all yourself," it may be important for you to learn to ask for and receive help in the healing process. However, "healing" and "cure" are not the same. In our society, we would like to see everyone cured of a disease. Death still seems to be a failure, even though on the logical level we know that everyone on this planet will die at some time.

My friend Jim had a gentle way about him, with a shy smile and very expressive eyes. He occasionally attended the AIDS support group I led, but told me he didn't want to attend all the time since he thought it might result in more of a focus on his dis–ease than he wanted. After not seeing Jim for a few months, I received a call from a friend of his telling me Jim was in the hospital and seemed close to death. He had a very high fever and was delirious. His father was there with him. But Jim didn't die that night. Instead, his fever broke, and he got better and better. His doctor couldn't even understand how he had come through this brush with death and was doing so well. When I talked to Jim about his experience, he remembered that during the delirium of the fever, he thought to himself, *I'm not even 30 years old yet—I'm not ready to die!* Within moments, the fever broke and his healing began.

Jim had an incredible 30th birthday celebration with lots of friends, balloons, and great food. About a year later, he began dealing with some old patterns around relationships and his health declined again. Back in the hospital, he was on an oxygen tank to help his breathing. Several friends were with him when he suddenly took off his oxygen mask. As they tried to persuade him to put it back on, Jim smiled and said "No, there are some men in a boat who are here to take me across the river. It's my time to go." He made his transition peacefully, surrounded by people who cared about him. At one point in his life, Jim chose life. At another point, it was time to leave.

Death is not a failure: it's a part of life, just like being born. Our Spirit is eternal. No matter how many vitamins and herbs you take, how often you exercise, or what your diet is, you will make your transition at some time. In the meantime, place your orders for health: mentally, physically, emotionally, and spiritually. Pay attention to the messages your body gives you. Learn to love and appreciate the vessel that houses your soul while you are on this planet.

Judy is a vibrant, enthusiastic, and very young 60 years old. If you were to meet her, you would never guess that at age 46 she was given a terminal diagnosis of Lou Gehrig's disease (ALS.) Both Judy's maternal grandmother and her mother had died of it, so when she began having initial symptoms, like weakness on her left side and vertigo, Judy thought, *I knew it, I knew it.* Her doctor basically told her to go enjoy life as best she could for the next few years, as there was no treatment. And yet, somewhere deep inside Judy knew she wanted to live. A few glimmers of hope appeared—a neurologist who was supportive and an article about a skier who kept active, despite a diagnosis of MS.

Judy went to her doctor and pleaded for an order for physical therapy. She began a three times a week, two–year regimen. During the therapy, her physical therapist gave her positive messages about getting well and simple visualizations, like: "See the muscles strengthened." Judy bought an anatomy book to study and began to visualize the journey of the thought, *leg move*, from brain to leg. Her mental attitude started changing. She studied nutrition and supplements and put together a program for herself. As the pieces of her healing came together and she began to improve, her doctor remarked that perhaps she had been misdiagnosed. However, there was a major revelation still waiting.

One beautiful day Judy and husband Tom went to their boat in Oxnard and discovered a metaphysical bookstore at a nearby marina. There was a small blue book and a tape on sale by someone Judy had never heard of: Louise Hay. As she looked through the book, she immediately knew: "If we can create it, we can uncreate it." Early the next day, she called Louise's publishing house and was referred to a women's support group. Although initially disappointed that Louise herself was not facilitating the group, the strong, beautiful black woman who was leading the group, Linda, was the perfect person to confront Judy and ask her, "What do you think this is about for you?" Defensive at first, Judy followed Linda's suggestion to see someone who could guide her through an intense breathing technique called "rebirthing" to get to the core issues.

The emotions she accessed during the rebirthing session exploded like a volcano. The sobs and anger and self–recrimination surfaced as she remembered the most traumatic experience of her life. In 1974, Judy had had an abortion. Although she and her soon–to–be husband felt there was no alternative at the time, to Judy she had taken a life and was in total shame about her decision, fearful that people would find out.

Once married, Judy thought having a child would release her guilt about the abortion, but her husband felt otherwise. When she realized there wouldn't be a child, the feelings of anger, sadness, and regret were forced deep within her, with a vow never to speak of them again. The healing release during the rebirthing began the journey of forgiveness she and her husband needed. Their relationship, along with Judy's health, began to heal and is stronger than ever.

Still fearful of others knowing what she had done, Judy courageously shared her story at the women's support group and was overwhelmed at the comfort and support she received. She told her two children from a previous marriage about the abortion, and they were also supportive. No longer needing to use energy to suppress the past, Judy could now allow the full healing to occur.

Every morning Judy began affirming, "Thank you, God, for this beautiful day and for every cell in my body doing its perfect job." She would imagine the perfection within and know that she was guided to do whatever was needed. She began visualizing herself in her kitchen with a red apron on, with her two (not yet born or even conceived) grandchildren asking for another chocolate chip cookie. She also visualized running a marathon (some of you, like me, are thinking—why?), something she had been training for before her diagnosis of ALS.

In March, 1989, at forty–eight years old, wearing number 48, Judy completed the Los Angeles mara-

thon in 5 hours, 43 minutes. While running the race,
she knew not only would she finish the race, but would
also live. During part of the race Judy felt like she was
flying, thanked God for being there. Jogging into the
stadium at the end of the race and seeing the Olympic
Flame, she knew that this day was the real beginning
of her mission on earth.

Before the race, the marathon committee had sent
out writers to interview this remarkable woman who
had been diagnosed with ALS and was running a marathon. After the articles were published, she began to
get calls from people with challenging illnesses. She
went to visit each one, sharing her story. She would
say, "What is this wake–up call about for you? Find
out and let it go. Move into the solution."

Judy continued taking workshops and classes and
is now an ordained minister in the City of Angels
Church of Religious Science in Los Angeles. She is a
shining presence, a testimonial, not just to the power
of affirmations and visualizations, but to the potential
for healing in all of us when we have the courage to
confront the deepest fears and secrets within us, forgive, and step out of the past into a radiant future.

What limiting ideas about your health and energy
do you want to release? What new beliefs do you want
to embrace? On the next page, read through the health
affirmations and really <u>feel</u> them. Following
on the next page, write out your own
healthy orders.

Affirmations for health:

Every cell in my body is alive with health and energy.

❖

My body is strong and healthy.

❖

Every system in my body functions exactly as it was intended to.

❖

I easily choose to nurture my body with healthy foods.

❖

I move and exercise my body in ways that feel good.

❖

My immune system is strong and healthy.

❖

I meditate daily to give my body deep rest and enhance my immune system.

❖

I breathe deeply, bringing energy to all my cells.

❖

My body is flexible.

❖

My body has a remarkable capacity for healing.

❖

Every resource I need for my healing comes to me.

❖

I am so grateful for the beautiful way the trillions of cells in my body work together!

❖

My Healthy Orders.....

Chapter 8

Relationship Orders

Michele is a tall, slender brunette with a great smile, lots of energy, and a delightful French accent. She is a talented and successful advertising woman from Canada. Her story about creating a relationship illustrates the power of letting go and looking inside for love instead of outside. Michele attended my training workshop in San Diego in 1999. In one of the awareness exercises, participants are led into a meditation and asked to identify a challenge or concern in their lives for which they need an answer. Following the meditation, their instructions are to go outside quietly and let nature give them the answer. After this exercise, people often reported dramatic insights into the real solution for their problems. (You can try this one, too.) After leaving the workshop room, Michele walked across the street to a small beach on an inlet to the San Diego harbor.

After some difficult relationships, she was affirming for a healthy, happy, intimate one, but nothing was happening. She asked herself, *What's the story with relationships in my life? What is the lesson? What is the challenge?* Suddenly a beautiful sailboat begged for her attention, the sail white against the perfect blue sky, birds flying high around its mast. It looked so graceful and free, sailing effortlessly across the channel, tacking back and forth with the wind. And then the answer dawned on her, and she wrote in her journal:

Release men. Let them go. Let go of the need. Like the bird, you are Michele, free. And so are men, free. Let all the men in your life be free. Let them express themselves just as they are. Release them all. And in the process, release yourself. Let yourself be 'free of needs.' You are doing good Michele, because just like the sailing boat that must tack back and forth to make its way to the open sea, you have been tacking back and forth to reach the open sea of love: yours. Love yourself, wonderful me. The perfect partner is there in the open sea.

Michele realized she needed to stop chasing love and learn to love herself first. She could let go of expectations and trust that her perfect partner would show up at the right time.

Seven months later Michele met Ron, to whom she is now engaged. And are you ready for this? Ron owns a beautiful 33' sailboat named Freedom!

Now, wouldn't it be terrific if we could all just sail away into the sunset like they do in the movies, and live happily ever after? Well, if you've been in an intimate relationship (are you on this planet?), you know that even when love endures, there are challenges that occur. As one of my mentors liked to say, "relationships are a cauldron of the hottest sauce in town!"

Although an intimate relationship with a life partner may be our most significant relationship, we have a whole range of relationships to work with: self, partner, family, friends, coworkers, and the thousands of people we encounter casually. So in this chapter, we're talking about the variety of relationships, not just our close intimate ones.

First and foremost, there is the relationship with yourself. When you look into your own eyes in the mirror, are you able to say "I love and approve of myself" and really believe it and feel it? Is there forgiveness work to do with yourself? You are a magnificent being with your own special place in the jigsaw puzzle of life. The more fully you're willing to love and approve of yourself, the more fully your energy can vibrate in the flow of the Universe. I believe that the healing of the individual is the basis of healing our planet. The planet needs YOU to love yourself. Are you willing to stop playing small?

Loving and accepting yourself exactly the way you are is also the key to great relationships with others. I know you've all heard this one before, but you can always learn to love yourself more deeply and fully. When you believe that you need someone else to love you to be OK, you'll always be disappointed because you will expect someone else to meet all your needs. Most people weren't taught to love themselves and have high self–esteem in childhood, so they really need to work on this in adulthood.

You must be willing to love and accept ALL your many parts, not just the parts you like. We all have parts of ourselves we judge or don't like, such as an addiction or some personality trait. But rejecting those parts only denies our own wholeness. The story of Kathy illustrates how the acceptance of an addiction can lead to radical transformation.

Kathy was an attractive blond with blue eyes, a shy smile—and a secret. She was bulimic, overeating and then throwing up three to four times a day. When she came to me for therapy, she had been doing this for years, except for one period of time when attending Overeaters Anonymous. The group support had been helpful, but she needed something more. Kathy had a boyfriend and wanted to get married and have a baby, but first she wanted to "get rid of this awful behavior." The first time I handed her a mirror and asked her to say, "I love and approve of you exactly the way you are," she burst into tears. How could she love herself when she had this uncontrollable behavior?

Gently, I explained to Kathy that the more she resisted the behavior and rejected this part of herself, the more strongly she was holding it. *A Course in Miracles* tells us that guilt actually holds a behavior and perpetuates it. Letting go of the guilt allows it to shift. I told Kathy that the focus of our work together would be on her learning to love and approve of herself. That first session, she looked at me with skepticism, but made an appointment to return anyway.

Over the next several months, Kathy began the process of forgiving herself, loving herself, and learning about affirmations and the Cosmic Kitchen. She struggled with her body image, because she was overweight despite the throwing up. When I told her she needed to love herself, even when she was throwing up over the toilet bowl, she shook her head in disbelief. Still, looking in the mirror and saying, "I love you" became easier. She began to feel more comfortable in her body and have more confidence in herself.

One day Kathy literally bounced into my office with eyes sparkling and an air of great excitement. Had her boyfriend proposed? No. Something more important had happened. While she had been throwing up a few days before, she finally said, "I love you, and it's OK." And she hadn't thrown up since! The journey from head to heart had happened. That moment of revelation changed Kathy's life forever. She continued the abstinence, and within a year she and her boyfriend were married. Shortly thereafter, she became pregnant and had a healthy baby boy. Loving herself not only enabled her to release a behavior she didn't want, it gave her a new sense of self for an effective relationship with a partner and a child.

What part of you do you need to love? Be gentle with yourself. Release the guilt and be willing to love ALL of you. Read the affirmations at the end of this chapter and be willing to believe them for yourself.

From a spiritual perspective, the way we meet people and interact with them is not a random process, but rather for some learning purpose. Some relationships are brief and others last a lifetime. From a psychological perspective, the beliefs and patterns about relationships are formed at a young age, between three and five, so to have effective ones later in life you need to understand the unconscious beliefs that were formed at those young ages. By combining these two perspectives, there is a significant opportunity for transforming the patterns.

What I've observed is that relationships REPLAY the patterns from childhood. This provides an opportunity for healing, as an inner part of us is always looking to heal the wounds of childhood. Your feelings are a guide in your journey to wholeness, and you can certainly use your feelings in the area of relationships. Often the issues have to do with fear of abandonment, lack of trust, and how to be close versus how to have space for yourself. Since these feelings are held in the unconscious part of you (remember the iceberg?), an understanding of your own issues along with affirmations is usually necessary for creating the type of relationships you want.

The most common thing people do to replay childhood issues is marry someone similar to mom or dad. Have you done that? Because the patterns are unconscious people don't recognize that in the beginning, or they'd never get together. Few women would decide to look for someone just like Dad. In the beginning there is the great swell of romantic love and the feeling that you have met your soulmate and will live happily ever after! Our society has done a great job of showing us unrealistic relationships in the movies and books, so it's a shock when issues start showing up.

Even though you may have good rapport with Mom and Dad today, if the Inner Child still carries anger, guilt, or fear from childhood, it's important to deal with the feelings. In unconscious relationships, people start blaming the other person and making it their fault when old wounds resurface. If you can learn to explore your OWN feelings and get to the core issue, the problem with your partner can often be resolved. If you're putting in an order to the Cosmic Kitchen for a great intimate relationship, but your model growing up was emotional distance, the result may be attracting someone where you're initially close, but with time the same feelings of distance occur. Hardville Hendrix wrote an excellent book called *Getting the Love You Want* that can really help to understand these patterns. Start affirming that you understand the limiting beliefs that affect your relationships, and with awareness of them, use specific affirmations to start changing them.

A woman in one of my groups began affirming for a more harmonious relationship with her boyfriend. Within a few weeks, he broke off the relationship, certainly not the outcome she intended. However, less than three months later she met another man with whom she was much more compatible. The "harmonious relationship" was created, just not in the way she expected. Remember that you can't control other people with affirmations, because they have their own set of beliefs and feelings. But the Cosmic Kitchen will take your order and fulfill it in the way that matches your request most closely.

The Universe doesn't just use intimate relationships for healing. Have you ever had a boss or friend who reminded you of someone you grew up with? When one of my clients realized that the issues with her boss were like those with her sister growing up, her perspective on the "problem" changed completely. She began affirming for a harmonious relationship with her boss and discovered that she could deal with the situation much differently.

Good communication is another key for improving our relationships since we can't expect others to read our minds. That would be very convenient, but it doesn't happen. And most of us weren't taught to speak up for ourselves in positive ways, so there's a whole learning process to learning how to communicate. You can begin affirming that you have more effective communication skills, and that you are guided in verbal interactions with your partner and others. Even when you don't know what to say, you can tell the other person how your body feels. For example, "I'm not sure what I want to say right now, but I can tell you my stomach feels like it's in a knot."

And then there is forgiveness, a most powerful process for shifting relationships. Chuck is an attractive gay man who attended some of my groups. His brother had shut off a relationship with him because he was gay. In the group one night, we were working with forgiveness, and Chuck decided "OK, one more time, I'll forgive my brother, not to change him, but to release ME." He only did his own forgiveness work, he didn't try to contact his brother. A few weeks later Chuck came to the group, and with tears in his eyes, read the letter of reconciliation from his brother. The energy of his forgiveness had gone out into the Cosmic Kitchen and brought back the gift of love.

Poet William Blake wrote the following short poem to his wife. "Throughout eternity, I forgive you and you forgive me." Forgiveness is a continual process, especially with those closest to us.

At times clients have asked, "How do you know when to stay in a relationship and when to leave?" If the relationship is abusive physically or emotionally, the answer is obvious: leave. If you really love yourself, you won't stay in an abusive situation. If the other person is willing to go to therapy, a separation while you're both in therapy could lead to some breakthroughs. But in most cases, there is no easy answer to this question. Affirm that you are guided in the right decision for you. At one of my work shops, a woman who had been thinking about leaving her husband showed me an affirmation about finding her soulmate. The affirmation didn't feel right, and I suggested she use the affirmation, "I have clarity about my current relationship." That one felt right to her because she had to resolve her feelings about her current partner as a first step in deciding about the future.

In my own marriage, there were conflicting feelings about whether to stay or go. My husband was a wonderful, supportive man and I truly loved him. We were best friends, but my spiritual path seemed to be pushing me to leave. After months of inner struggle, the message during meditation was, "Just be at peace. You will know what to do at the right time." And when the time came to separate, my husband also knew it was the right thing to do. We were able to cry together, and appreciate the time we had been together. We have remained friends, and even met each other's new partners.

Some books you read will suggest that you make a list of everything you want in a partner. For a while I did this, but it didn't feel right. I decided there were certain qualities that were really important to me, and that I would let Spirit bring whatever relationships were needed for my development. The qualities that were (and are) primary for me included: dedication and passion for the spiritual path; an open, loving heart; good communication; and a good sense of humor. But when the Universe filled that order, I wasn't quite ready for what seemed lacking!

Just before one of my trips to England to lead a workshop, about six years after my divorce, I went into the church bookstore to purchase angel pins to give my assistants. After a wonderful conversation with the volunteer there, Rick Nichols, I walked out thinking, "*what a nice man.*" Little did I know at the time that the bookstore manager had told Rick about me and suggested he take me out.

Two days later, literally walking out my front door on the way to the airport, heavy green suitcase in hand, the phone rang. Hesitating for a moment, I decided to answer it. It was Rick, asking me to donate a few tickets for my upcoming mind/body workshop at the church as one of the prizes for the Casino Night he was organizing. There was a plane to catch, so I was rather abrupt, and said, "Sure, whatever, fine with me," and took off for the airport.

About six weeks later, the day for my mind/body

workshop arrived. I was scheduled to speak briefly at both services to promote the workshop, so I found a seat near the front of the church where it would be easy to walk onto the platform. I looked up and there was Rick, on the platform to give the announcements. In that moment I KNEW he was the one—and immediately panicked. Getting what you want can sometimes be scary!

The workshop room that afternoon was filled to overflowing, but somehow, after starting the mind/body video after the break, the only seat left was next to Rick. We talked briefly after the workshop, and he suggested I come by the bookstore when he was volunteering. Not wanting to look too obvious, I waited until Tuesday. (Isn't love silly sometimes?) We finally went out for coffee, and that's when I discovered he had no job and no money. He survived by doing odd jobs and trading volunteer time in the bookstore for a room with the manager and her husband. We went out a few more times (to free things) and then I decided it was time to have a serious talk with God. "God, OK, you sent me this guy with my most important qualities, but I never expected that he wouldn't have a job. What's the deal?" The answer was "This is not a problem." "Listen God, maybe you didn't hear me. I said thanks for those important qualities, but he doesn't have any money!" And God replied quite clearly, "Excuse me, you didn't hear ME. THIS IS NOT A PROBLEM."

Well, that was certainly clear. I decided to trust

my feelings and God's answers, and let the relationship develop. Within a short time I realized it wasn't
a problem. Rick had been in very responsible jobs
for many years, and had decided to take some time
off to pursue a spiritual path and develop himself
quickly. Indeed, he had courage to take the road less
traveled. And as time went by, he brought tremendous creativity to my business, creating web–sites, a
newsletter, and beautiful brochures. He began co–
leading workshops with me, bringing his own wisdom to them, and then creating his own speaking
career. We have become wonderful partners, in love,
life, and business.

Relationships with ourselves and others are very
precious. They provide an avenue for tremendous
growth in our capacity for love and compassion. What
do you want to affirm for in the relationships in your
life? Read the ones on the following
page and then create your own.

Affirmations for relationships:

I approve of myself.

❖

I love and accept <u>all</u> parts of myself.

❖

Loving myself heals my life.

❖

I express my feelings openly and easily.

❖

I forgive myself and others totally.

❖

I am willing to accept love. I deserve love.

❖

*I am aware of past patterns that no longer serve
me and release them easily.*

❖

*I listen closely and open my heart when
interacting with others.*

❖

The love I extend returns to me multiplied.

❖

*I enjoy wonderful associations with positive, uplifting
people.*

❖

I love and appreciate the members of my family.

❖

My relationships are filled with joy and fun and love.

My Relationship Orders.....

I welcome fun and travel orders from the Cosmic Kitchen. It's exciting to travel to new and exotic places. I enjoy creating my Treasure Map and having manifestations show up at exactly the right time.

Chapter 9

Traveling orders, Fun Orders, and Treasure Maps

Have fun with your orders to the Cosmic Kitchen! In the first stages of practice, people often affirm for good parking spaces. That's fine, but be willing to go for a lot more. What else would add ease and fun to your life? Let's look at some examples of fun orders.

My organizer in the UK, Norma Jarvis, and one of my assistants, Jackie Turner, went to Ireland to look at venues for a course there. On the way home, they stayed one night at a hotel at the Dublin Airport. Norma had never had room service before, so she called and ordered a meal. The hotel person said it would take a half–hour, but after thirty minutes, no meal, so Norma called again. "Oh, we're sorry we didn't pass on the message, your meal will be there in 15 minutes." As Jackie and Norma sat chatting, Norma suddenly opened her arms and said, "I am open and receptive to all good." At that moment, there was a knock on the door. The waiter appeared with her meal and said "No charge!"

A few years following my divorce, Valentine's Day was approaching, but this particular year I wasn't seeing anyone. Still, I thought it would be so nice to get flowers for Valentine's Day. I began affirming to receive flowers. Well, Feb. 14th came and went—no flowers! A few days later when I arrived home after a conference, there was a message on my answerphone: "No matter how late you get in, come into the office and get the beautiful flowers that arrived for you!" The office wasn't far from my home, so I jumped in the car and drove there. The bouquet was a dozen beautiful yellow roses sent by one of my clients who was very appreciative of a break–through he had made in a session that week. Once again, the Universe brought me my order from a very unexpected source.

Treasure Maps are a fun, visual way to place your orders in all areas with the Cosmic Kitchen. To get started, collect the following: a large piece of poster board; some magazines with themes of health, success, travel, and spiritual growth; a pair of scissors; crayons or colored pencils; and a glue stick. Block out 2 or 3 hours. Invite like–minded friends over to create their own Treasure Maps. Then go through the magazines and cut out pictures and phrases that represent what you are ordering for your life. Include ALL areas of your life. So even if you're healthy, still include some pictures and phrases for optimum health.

Find pictures and words or phrases that represent the wonderful relationships you desire, the vibrant health, the travel destinations, the spiritual connection, the perfect career, and the financial prosperity you're ordering. When you have all the pictures and words you want, glue everything on the poster board and create a montage. Add in additional words or affirmations with the colored pencils. Have fun and be outrageous! Imagine the most fabulous life you can and put it in the Treasure Map. If you're doing this with some friends, give everyone time to show their Treasure Map and talk about what they're creating. One rule: everyone in the group must give complete support for everything on each Treasure Map. No judgments about whether or not something is possible. Then hang your Treasure Map somewhere where you can see it every day, but not in the living room where everyone coming to your home would see it. People who do not believe in the possibilities of life may try to "rain on your parade." Only share your Treasure Map with those you know are supportive. And then enjoy the miracles that happen!

As the orders on my Treasure Map are filled, I want to put up new orders. So I add them to my existing Treasure Map for a while, and then every year or so, I create a completely new one. My Treasure Maps always include a picture of the world and a list of places where I want to travel.

My favorite vacation spots in the world are the Hawaiian Islands. When I was married, we made several trips to Hawaii, visiting the islands of Oahu, Kauai, and Maui. One night in 1992 I attended a seminar at my church with Terry Cole–Whittaker, a well–known spiritual and metaphysical speaker. During her talk on abundance, Terry said, "everyone's always affirming for money. Why don't you just affirm directly for what you want?" That idea really clicked with me, so after the seminar I started thinking, *What do I want to affirm for?* The answer came quickly, *A free vacation to Hawaii.* For the next few months, I would occasionally think my affirmation, *It is so exciting to have a free week in Hawaii.* I would feel great gratitude to the Universe for arranging this vacation.

One day I happened to be talking with an acquaintance and she mentioned that she had just been to Hawaii for a conference on guided imagery. Causally, I asked her where she liked to stay when she went there, and she replied, "Oh, my husband and I are part–owners in a condominium on Kauai. I'd love for you to go there for a week as my guest. I appreciate the help you've given me in the past." Wow—it is always so amazing how the Universe works things out. But the story doesn't stop there. It took a few months before the actual week was scheduled. In the meantime, I asked the man I was dating at the time if he would like to come to Hawaii with me. After he said yes, I started affirming for free airline tickets. But for some reason, despite all the affirmations I had seen work, doubting self–talk started in my mind, and so we ended up paying for our tickets.

The day came to fly to Hawaii. We were excited and happy as we got on the plane. About halfway through the flight, my friend said to me, "You know, I just realized I probably have enough frequent flyer miles for us to have gotten free tickets." I looked at him in disbelief. I wasn't sure whether to throw him or myself off the plane! It was so clear that I had accepted my good at one point and then denied it at another. This experience taught me to stay with my Cosmic orders and let the Kitchen figure out how to fulfill them. As you'll see from the next story, LoAnne did that beautifully.

LoAnne is a beautiful soul, inside and out. She has a gentle, loving energy, and people feel good just being around her. For many years, she has held classes in her home to teach people many of the ideas in this book. As she was contemplating her sixtieth birthday, the idea to celebrate it in Paris popped up. She began affirming "I celebrate my birthday in Paris at a price I can easily afford." This became her walking mantra. She visualized herself at a restaurant at the Eiffel Tower having a birthday celebration and enjoying every moment. She asked others to visualize her there.

Balancing action and affirmations, she wrote to her alma mater to see if any graduates were living in Paris.

There were, so she wrote to them. One answered her letter, and she was offered a free place to stay in Paris, starting on August 1st. However, her birthday was actually on July 28th, so she decided to book a hotel for the first few days. A travel agent neighbor just "happened" to stop by her house, and gave her a recommendation for a small, reasonably priced hotel, plus the name of a tour company.

Next were the airline reservations. She continued affirming "I celebrate my birthday in Paris at a price I can easily afford." On the suggestions of friends, LoAnne checked the points on her visa card and discovered she had enough for her and her husband's tickets, even enough to upgrade to First Class. Before arriving at the airport, they were only able to get on the upgrade list. They visualized being together in First Class, and so it came to pass.

Once settled into their lovely little hotel, the tour company arranged dinner at the Eiffel Tower and a boat ride on the Seine for LoAnne's birthday, a truly joyous occasion. On August 1st, they moved to their two bedroom apartment for the rest of their stay, feeling blessed to live "as Parisians." The actual outcome of her affirmation to celebrate her birthday in Paris at a price she could easily afford far exceeded her expectations.

What fun and traveling orders would you like to send to the Cosmic Kitchen? Use the next page to create your affirmations.

My Traveling Orders.....

My Fun Orders.....

I am delighted to be living in my perfect home. It is a wonderful, nurturing space with all the amenities that are important to me. It is filled with joy, beauty, and love.

Chapter 10

Housing Orders

What do you like about where you live now? Is there anything you would like to change? You spend the majority of your time in your home (unless you travel a great part of the time), and you deserve to have a place that's attractive to you physically, emotionally, and spiritually. Make a list of everything you want in a home. Open your imagination.

When my ex–husband and I bought our first home, I had been meditating for a few years, but didn't yet know consciously about using affirmations. We had a few requirements in mind, like three bedrooms, and a price we could afford, but nothing else. Our idea of a price we could easily afford was about $34,000. (Can you imagine prices this low? This was back in the mid–seventies.) We told the real estate agent our price range, and she began taking us to houses that were over $40,000. They were lovely, but too far out of range. So, we asked if there were any "fixer–uppers" that we could look at. The agent looked skeptical, probably because my husband was disabled from a bout with polio at age two, and he didn't look like he would be able to do much work on a house, but we persisted with the idea. She had no idea how resourceful my husband was. She took us to a fixer–upper, and we were delighted, despite the obvious need for a lot of work on the house. It had two bedrooms and a den, a good–sized living room with a small area for a dining table, a TV room, AND a pool and a guesthouse, all for $35,000! Now that was a bargain. With a lot of hard work over the next four years, the house was transformed. The following year we decided it was time to sell it and move back toward the beach. Our first house was located in a very hot, smoggy area of California, and I vowed not to spend another summer in a place where the smog was so bad that during the summer you couldn't even see the mountains that were only a few miles away.

This time we KNEW about affirmations, and listed everything we wanted—including the fact that the house would be beautiful and ready to occupy. Fixing up had been fine for the first house, but we were ready to do less work and enjoy more. On the very first day of looking, we found the perfect house in a quiet, lovely neighborhood. It was newly painted, with a beautiful carpet, lots of open space, and a price we could easily afford.

Even children can place their orders with the Cosmic Kitchen. Lilly was ten years old when she told her parents, Elizabeth and John–Paul, "I want a room like Mitras'." Her parents told Lilly that besides the fact that they weren't even thinking about moving, the neighborhood Lilly was talking about seemed a little out of their price range. They forgot about Lilly's order.

A few years later Elizabeth and John–Paul were driving home from church and saw an Open House sign. Elizabeth had been walking in the mornings in that neighborhood and had thought how nice it would be to live there. They sat in the house for two hours, which had been vacant for seven months. They had wanted a house that called to them, with no long hunt, and this one seemed to be doing that. The next week they took Lilly to see the house. When she walked inside, Lilly exclaimed, "Mom, this is Mitras' house!"

"Don't you mean this is like Mitras' house?" asked Elizabeth.

"No, this was Mitras' house and now I'll have her room!" said Lilly. Their family has now been happily living in that home for more than three years.

When doing your affirmations, remember to include "this or something better" because the Universe may have a grander plan than you have. Margaret and her husband Mike left the flat they owned in St. Albans, England, and moved to another town when Mike took a new job. Margaret was affirming that the flat was rented out quickly and easily, but nothing was happening. They even invented Mr. and Mrs. Trustworthy as the ideal tenants. Then one day she wrote out: "Our flat is rented out or something better happens. All is well in my world." Within two weeks they had an offer to buy the flat, definitely their idea of something better.

Right now, I am living in a beautiful home located on seven acres (three of them with avocado trees) in north San Diego County. Even with all the affirmation and visualization work I've done, I'd never envisioned a place like this. Rick and I moved here in 1998 from a 1400 square foot condo. Now THAT is a change. We didn't even own a rake.

When Rick and I met, my home was a lovely condominium bought after my divorce. The living room faced a small man–made lake with a waterfall, and there were vaulted ceilings with a small loft upstairs that was perfect for meditation. When moving in, I had fixed it up EXACTLY as I wanted it, to consciously change the old belief from childhood that I had to settle for less because the best was too expensive.

While the condo was perfect for me as a single woman, Rick and I together wanted something different. We wanted some land to plant flowers and an extra bedroom for a guestroom, and rooms for separate offices. (Rick loves to sing and talk while working and I like quiet.) The need to move wasn't urgent, so we started just paying attention to homes we liked as we were out on the weekends. We began collecting flyers for homes and putting them on our dream board. We really let our imagination soar, because all the homes we liked were large and expensive, priced between $750,000 and a million dollars. Our income wasn't even close enough to purchase one of these homes unless we won the lottery, but we kept knowing that the Universe would lead us to the perfect home.

One weekend we were in San Diego and spontaneously decided to look at some of the open houses listed in the Sunday paper. That first day we found a fabulous real estate agent. She partnered with a wonderful loan agent. Using the left–brain accountant skills inherited from my parents, I quickly calculated that we could afford a house in a certain price range, and it wasn't even close to the houses we had on our dream board. But we got excited about looking, and our agent began taking us to different properties. She listened carefully to what each of us wanted and did her best to find places that included our priorities. We saw some spectacular places with huge family rooms and gorgeous master baths, but the perfect place hadn't yet appeared. As our house hunting continued, we were going farther and farther out into the country in north San Diego county.

Here are the affirmations we were using:

We have our perfect home in a wonderful location at a price we can easily afford. We have the best combination of fabulous view and fantastic house at an excellent price. Spirit guides us to the perfect place. The house has a lovely energy. It has everything we want, including at least four bedrooms and space for workshops. We have more than enough money for the down–payment, escrow, and any other new house needs we have. The condo sells at an excellent price and both escrows close at just the right time.

There was one property we looked at several times. It had most of what we wanted, and we decided to sign the papers for an offer. But that night when we got home Rick told me, "We have to look one more day." What? I was NOT a happy camper. I told him he had to call our agent, as I was not about to tell her to find some additional places to look.

The next weekend we looked again, joined by our friend Verity, who was visiting from Barbados. Nothing we saw all morning changed my mind about the property we were already considering, and I was getting tired and cranky. We stopped at a little hamburger stand to get some lunch. The stand was named Nessy Burgers, after the Loch Ness monster. Set on a two–lane road in a little town named Bonsall, it was certainly a strange place to be named after a monster supposedly spotted in Scotland. At that moment, I had no idea we would be living only a few miles from Nessy Burgers within three months.

After lunch we continued our search. Finally, we were approaching the last house on the list, driving along a winding two–lane road with mountain views and avocado groves and flower farms. The scenery was beautiful, and Rick commented, "I could live out here." Spontaneously, I replied, "You just might have to."

The private street down to the house was steep, barely wide enough for two cars, and lined with avocado trees. As we drove down the driveway to the house, we saw an incredible view out over a small valley, with Mt. Palomar off in the distance. Just looking at the view created a sense of peace. There were a few orange, lemon, and lime trees right by the driveway, and—there were three acres of avocado trees. Wow—guacamole whenever we wanted it. (What I didn't know at the time was that Rick had always wanted an avocado grove, and had almost bought one years before we met. The Cosmic Chef never forgets a strong order!)

But when I walked into the house, the wow stopped. Inside, we found not four, but five bedrooms, a huge loft where at least twenty people would fit for workshops, a 30' x 18' living/dining area, and four bathrooms. Plus a garage with space for Rick to lead his fountain–making workshops. Sounds great, doesn't

it? Except that I didn't like the inside. Despite all
the space, it was crowded with mismatched furniture, many of the walls were paneled with unfinished
rough wood, the kitchen was that 1970's burnt orange, the master bedroom bath needed lots of work,
the carpet needed replacing (and this was a BIG
house) and there were papers and boxes piled every-
where. Because I'm so kinesthetic, it didn't "feel"
good to me. To me, it felt claustrophobic. It seemed
like a fixer–upper, and I had vowed never to buy a
fixer–upper again. Plus, I wondered if the current
owners would really be able to clear everything out
and actually move.

To Rick it was the perfect place. We quickly went
upstairs, and outside on a small deck was a swing.
We sat in the swing looking out at the view, and it
certainly felt good and peaceful there. Downstairs,
Verity was already deciding which bedroom would
be my office.

We left with Rick convinced that this was indeed,
THE house. With his vision, he was seeing the house
as it could be, not as it was. And the view didn't need
any changing. It was, and is, quite spectacular. Soon
I realized (Rick is very persuasive) that with paint
and new carpet downstairs, and knocking out one wall
to enlarge the master bedroom, the house would be
wonderful. The other remodeling could be done later.
So we called our agent to make the offer. Incredibly,
the price for the house and seven acres was about
the same as a modest three bedroom home in the

area from which we were moving. To us, it became our million–dollar house at a price we could easily afford. This was a powerful example of dreaming big and letting the Cosmic Kitchen find the perfect fulfillment of our order at the right time. We know Spirit guided us to this property. In fact, it had been on the market for ten months with no offers, just waiting for us.

On the next page, write out affirmations for your ideal home. Remember, you deserve to live in a place that is wonderful and nurturing.

My Housing Orders....

Chapter 11

When the Kitchen Gives You Lemons

Regardless of how many affirmations and visualizations you do, there will be some challenges in your life. Why? Because the path of soul development needs challenges to grow. Growing beautiful flowers takes sun, water—and manure. Growing beautiful souls takes mental, emotional, and spiritual nurturing—and challenges. If there were no challenges, how would you be motivated to grow and change? A crisis in career, health, finances, or a relationship provides a wake–up call to stop and examine your life.

I've experienced a divorce, a chronic illness, failing exams for my professional work, and a lawsuit (plus all the usual little stuff.) Some of my challenges have felt like the kitchen sent me lemons, while others have felt like a whole load of manure was dumped on my doorstep. While going through these difficult experiences I was sustained by my connection with Spirit. Each challenge taught me something important about myself, about life, and about trusting the process of change. Studying *A Course in Miracles* has brought an incredible sense of peace with all the changes that occur in life, as it is a reminder that I am Spirit, and that is the only reality that endures.

When in private practice, I often told my clients, "follow your heart or the Universe will kick you in the butt and then you'll be forced to move." (Of course, I was telling myself the same thing.) So, when one of my clients who had been complaining for months about his job, but kept resisting looking for another one, came in and said he had been fired, I said "Hallelujah! The Universe has just kicked your butt. You can stop complaining about that job and I can stop hearing your complaints." He decided to pursue his dream of moving to San Francisco, and within three weeks he had found a job and an affordable place to live there, something he had previously said couldn't be done.

For the past ten years a remarkable woman named Odile has been the Program Director at the Inside Edge, the morning group I wrote about in the career chapter. Originally from South Africa, she has an elegant presence and charming accent. As Program Director, Odile has brought in weekly speakers to the Inside Edge, many of them well–known authors. She has a knack for booking thought–provoking and inspirational speakers on the cutting edge of personal and planetary growth. Her path to this position began with her getting fired.

After six months of working at a glitzy advertising and PR firm, Odile knew it was not a fit with her values, plus her duties at the firm weren't what she had expected. But—there was an inner conflict because the money was good and she didn't want to let go of that. Every night, she began praying with an open–ended affirmation for divine guidance and her highest and best good, especially in the area of work.

A few days after returning from a week–long vacation, the woman who managed Odile called her into her office, and abruptly said, "This is your last day." In shock, Odile left, thinking, "Oh, my God, I'm not good enough." But another part of her was elated, knowing this was the answer to her affirmation. She had been thinking about starting her own PR firm, and here was the opportunity. Quickly she made up business cards and letterhead, and soon had several clients.

Within a year she was offered two positions that fit her spiritual values. The first was the position of editor for the 16–page newspaper for a large church, and the second, following just six months later, was the position of Program Director at the Inside Edge. She worked as a consultant in both positions and later released just the editor position to focus on her love of art and continue as Program Director.

Think about it—when has the Universe forced you to move when you didn't want to? What was the result? If you stopped resisting, the result was probably good. If you tried to hold on, it most likely became more difficult. A wonderful book about the process of change is called *Who Moved My Cheese?* by Spencer Johnson, M.D.

During times of change, it's also helpful to reach out to others for support. In my workshops, I often ask, "How many of you have difficulty asking for help?" Almost all the hands go up. Then I ask, "How many of you would be happy to support a friend who needed help?" Usually all hands go up. While willing to give, many were reluctant to ask for what they needed. Then we discuss how asking for what you need is an important part of loving yourself.

There have been times in my life when I've followed my heart and intuition before the Universe had to give me a kick, and other times when I didn't (and wished I had.) One time when I didn't was while working as a psychological intern. It seemed "logical" that I pursue getting licensed as a psychologist, which involves written and oral exams. Although my heart wasn't really in it, I started studying and registered for the national written exam. For me, multiple choice exams were always a snap, so I passed with a very high percentage on the first try. The next step was taking the state oral exam. It doesn't sound too difficult: twenty minutes with a panel of two people asking questions about a case history you had a few minutes to read. Well, it was grueling. Feeling humiliated and depressed, I left the first oral exam knowing I had failed. Because my Ph.D. degree was in social psychology, not clinical psychology, even my experience as an intern wasn't sufficient to make up for the clinical courses missed. Yes, I was doing affirmations, but the energy behind them was never 100%.

Did I listen to my heart? No—after taking some special short "catch–up" courses, I kept trying to pass the exam, not once, but three more times. Driving home after the fourth time, again knowing failure, it was clear it was time to stop pushing myself to pass the exam. What a relief! But now what? I could stay on as an intern forever (oh, dreadful thought) or go on a different path. My decision that day led me to the most rewarding work I have done so far—conducting international training workshops that prepare people to lead spiritually–based workshops on the principles in this book.

However, while making the transition from intern to workshop leader, my income dipped considerably. Although I was affirming for a certain income per month, it wasn't happening. My fear level began increasing, along with credit card debt. Why weren't my affirmations working this time? Meditating one December morning, I affirmed to understand what was going on. The clear message was this: "Trust. Be patient. Everything will turn around in July." July seemed a long time away at that moment, but from many previous experiences in my life, I knew that Spirit was guiding me, and that everything would turn around. And in July, it did.

Remember the iceberg? A natural part of life is the continual process of becoming aware of unconscious beliefs, because they will create things you may not want until you become aware of them. For example, my mother experienced a divorce after being married for thirty–one years. This was the most painful time of her life. When I was the same age she had been at the time of the divorce, a very difficult experience related to my career occurred in my life. It was months before I realized that after watching my mother's process I had developed the belief "you can have a wonderful life for many years and then unexpected challenges happen." Despite the discomfort of the experience, it also spurred me to expand my career in new ways, this book being one of them. Challenge always holds within it the potential for breakthroughs in heart and mind.

Change is a part of life. The more quickly you adapt, the more quickly you'll find happiness. Letting go and surrendering to what is happening rather than resisting it allows you to step into your next level. This doesn't mean you won't feel sadness, anger, or betrayal. When you have those feelings, it's important to feel them and process them, but not to hold onto them. Holding on will keep you stuck. A dog named Jasmine taught me a valuable lesson about letting go.

Jasmine, an eleven–year–old yellow lab, belonged to my personal assistant, Stef. While Stef answered my phone calls and emails, Jasmine sprawled happily on a huge pillow in the office. Part of the employee package was that Jasmine received a big new rawhide bone every week. Often there would be just a small nub of one left at the end of the week. The next week, Jasmine would resume chewing on the small nub when Stef brought in a new bone. Did Jasmine eagerly let go of the old to receive the new? No! Only with much coaxing could Stef entice her to finally let go of the old nub. Perhaps you've had an experience like that, too, where you held onto something old because you couldn't trust that the new would be even better.

One of my favorite metaphors for stepping out in faith comes from a wonderful scene in the movie, *Indiana Jones and the Last Crusade*. Indiana is on a quest for the Holy Grail (the chalice Jesus drank from at the Last Supper.) The quest becomes truly urgent when Indiana's father is shot, and only the water from the Grail will save him. Using a small book with ambiguous clues, Indiana passes two obstacles and arrives at the third, a huge crevice resembling the Grand Canyon. His only clue is to "leap from the lion's head." To do so appears to be falling to his death in the abyss. His inner struggle is apparent as the camera shows the close–up of his face. Does he trust the clue and leap or not? Suddenly, he leaps! Incredibly, there is a bridge he lands on that was invisible before.

Life is like this. Spirit always has a safety net waiting for us. In the midst of a challenge, it can be difficult to really feel that there is a solution already in Divine Mind. And yet, the key is focusing on what you want, not what you're experiencing. I once heard philosopher and futurist Jean Houston say, "Depression is not the medium of miracles." How true. The medium of miracles is trusting that there is some solution for the challenge you're facing, even when you have no idea how it will happen. Focus on the result you want, not the challenge. Remember that what you resist persists. Most people have an old pattern of obsessing about the problem rather than ordering the solution from the Cosmic Kitchen. The more you obsess about the problem, the more strongly The Law of Attraction holds it in your life. When you focus on trusting that Spirit has a solution, the Law of Attraction can bring you the solution.

What helps <u>you</u> shift from fear and anxiety to trust? Perhaps it's reading a spiritual text or listening to an inspirational tape, or dancing to your favorite music. Perhaps it's watching children at the park or taking a walk in nature. Whatever it is, do it. And do it every day, not just when you are in crisis. We all have a tendency to wait until crisis strikes to turn to our spiritual source. (As they say, there are no atheists in foxholes.) Why wait? Get intimate with Spirit: feel the Power and Presence you are a part of <u>now</u>.

On the next page are some affirmations to help you deal with any challenge you're experiencing in your life at the moment. On the following page, write out your own affirmations. What words will help you feel more peaceful and trusting?

Affirmations for times of challenge:

*In this moment, I know that Spirit has
the solution to any concern in my life.*

❖

*I know the Cosmic Chef is preparing
the perfect dish to handle this situation.*

❖

I sleep in peace and wake in joy.

❖

*I breathe in and fill my body with trust. I breathe
out and let go of my concerns.*

❖

*I focus on this moment, and stay fully
present to the NOW.*

❖

*I am guided perfectly in any action I need
to take now.*

❖

I easily reach out to friends for support.

❖

I ask for the help I need and know I deserve help.

*I am joyfully trusting the Universe to create
the perfect outcome.*

❖

I easily listen to and trust my intuition.

❖

*I am joyfully and gratefully receiving miracles
in my life right now!*

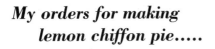

***My orders for making
lemon chiffon pie.....***

*With great joy I welcome the opportunity
to make wonderful changes in my life
that will have positive effects for the
entire planet. I am a pioneer in the
revolution to change the outer aspects of
life by starting within myself.*

Chapter 12

Imagine the Possibilities

Throughout history there have been voices that believed our thoughts create our experience.

"Our life is what our thoughts make it."
Marcus Aurelius, 1st century.
" As ye think so shall ye be."
Proverbs
" A man is just about as happy as he makes up his mind to be."
Abraham Lincoln

And yet most people still act and speak as though life is random and they are simply pawns in a huge chess game with unknown players. It's somehow easier to believe that forces "out there" are responsible for your life rather than your own inner thoughts and feelings. However, the stories and principles in this book have demonstrated that you <u>do</u> have a choice—to use your thoughts and feelings either to help you or keep you stuck. There is a Cosmic Kitchen ready and willing to fulfill your orders to experience a life greater than you have ever imagined.

Our world has experienced many dramatic changes in beliefs throughout the centuries. Galileo discovered that the earth revolved around the sun rather than vice versa, but was forced to recant or face death. Just over 500 years ago, people really believed they would fall off the edge of the earth if they sailed too far. Before 1916, people believed that we couldn't fly, much less go to the moon and beyond. In 1920 someone wanted to close the patent office because he believed everything that could be invented had already been invented. Perhaps we are on the verge of another true shift, one that recognizes the power of our own inner beliefs to change our outer reality. In the early twentieth century, the famous American psychologist William James said, "The greatest revolution of our generation is the discovery that human beings, by changing the inner attitudes of their minds, can change the outer aspects of their lives." How wonderful it is that human beings have a unique creative mind, a mind that is linked with Infinite Intelligence and Creativity!

It does take conscious commitment to stay aware of your thoughts and words when you first begin practicing the ideas in this book. Set aside some time every day, even a few minutes, to read the sample affirmations in different chapters and to write your own. Write them out on index cards and place them around your home and at work as a reminder of your new way of thinking. Record your affirmations on tape and play them to yourself. Sing them in your car on the way to work, and dance them in your living room. When you practice, you are literally creating new grooves in your brain. Perhaps your first affirmation could be, "I easily find time to create and practice my affirmations on a daily basis."

Affirmations and visualizations are techniques for creating more of what you want in your life, material things and careers as well as joy, peace, and love, the true sweetness of life. They are not meant to be used to control others. Indeed, you can't control others with your affirmations. But as you continue your affirmations and visualizations, the people with whom you need to connect are brought into your life.

As you are redesigning your life, it's important for you to feel joyful when you see or meet others who have what you want. If someone has a wonderful relationship, be happy for that person. If someone has created a marvelous career or excellent prosperity, be willing to learn from that person about the process. Remember that there is enough for everyone. Someone else having their ideal career doesn't prevent you from creating yours. We're all meant to be fulfilled, not just a select few. When you support others in their dreams and applaud their accomplishments, you are supporting yourself.

Every action begins with a thought. Many of them are not really conscious, such as moving your legs to walk or your hands to type. Every thought is energy. Energy flows where attention goes. When you give your attention to negative conditions, the energy of the negative is increased. When you give your attention to the positive, that energy is increased. This is true in your own life and also in the collective life of the planet.

We can also use affirmations and visualizations to help solve the challenges that face our society and our planet. When I was coming of age in the sixties, people were against the war, racism, and gender inequality. There were demonstrations and confrontations and finger pointing at those who seemed to be perpetuating these wrongs. But what I've learned through the study of affirmations is that to be against something actually mobilizes it more strongly. We must focus on being *for* peace rather than against war, *for* equal opportunity, *for* environmental protection, *for* equality between men and women, and *for* any other change we want to see in the world. When you make the "other person" or the "other country" or the "other group" the problem, you actually help polarize the differences more strongly. Instead of hating those who disagree with you, learn to accept that people have different viewpoints. Affirm for ways to live in harmony together. Coyotes taught Rick and me a valuable lesson about this.

Because we live out in the country, there are all manner of critters, including rabbits, gophers, squirrels, and coyotes. Rick had laid several hundred feet of tubing to carry water down to the flowers around the labyrinth we built. As the weather became warmer, the coyotes were looking for water and began chewing through the tubing almost daily. This meant Rick had to take time to go make repairs over and over. One day I affirmed there was a solution that would benefit us all. Soon the idea came—to put out a bowl of water for the coyotes so they wouldn't have to chew through the rubber. Rick took this idea a step further and put bowls in two places where they could be "watered" from the tubing when the flowers received their daily drink. With this solution, only one repair was needed over several months. Solutions for the world's challenges may be more complicated than this, but the principle is the same: focus on creating a solution for the good of all.

In 1986 John Randolph Price wrote a beautiful World Healing Meditation, based on the idea that our collective consciousness makes a difference. Each year on December 31st at noon Greenwich time, tens of thousands of people around the world participate in this meditation. Although the vision in the meditation has not yet been accomplished, there is socio-logical research suggesting that greater peace and harmony are created as more people meditate. In his book, *A New Science of Life*, Rupert Sheldrake pro-poses the idea of a morphogenic field that contains the collection of all thoughts. According to him, as the thoughts of peace in this field increase, the real-ity of peace will follow. Perhaps the morphogenic field is just another name for the Cosmic Kitchen.

Quantum physics supports the idea that every change creates an effect, like ripples in a pond spread-ing outward when a rock is thrown in. There was a fascinating physics experiment reported by Time magazine: two negative electrons were shot out of an accelerator and sent in different directions. One of them was then changed to a positive particle, and the other then spontaneously changed to positive. I like to think this is a metaphor for all of us. You are free to change your thoughts at any time, and that produces a new effect. Life is such a precious gift. Give yourself the gift of choosing life–affirming thoughts about yourself and the planet at any mo-ment.

Recently Rick and I sat in wonder on our deck, watching hundreds of shooting stars as the earth passed through the tail of a comet. Our own lives may seem small when compared to the vastness of the cosmos, but our own life is the only place we have to start living the kind of life we want. While there is much more to be explored in our outer world, to me the exploration and understanding of the inner world is truly the most important frontier, and will bring great wisdom to use in the outer world.

I wish you great joy and fun as you create your orders and receive them from the Cosmic Kitchen!

All the resources I need for my mental, emotional, and spiritual health and well-being come to me quickly and easily. I am blessed with all that I need for my growth and expansion.

Recommended Resources

My List of Terrific Books.........

SPIRITUAL GROWTH AND BASIC PRINCIPLES

A Course in Miracles

Gawain, Shakti, *Creative Visualization; Living in the Light*

Hay, Louise, *You Can Heal Your Life; The Power is Within You*

Holmes, Ernest, *Basic Ideas of Science of Mind*

Jampolsky, Gerald, *Love is Letting Go of Fear*

Shinn, Frances Scovill, *The Game of Life and How to Play It*

Williamson, Marianne, *A Return to Love*

HEALTH

Benson, Herbert, M.D., *The Relaxation Response; Maximum Mind*

Borysenko, Joan, Ph.D., *Minding the Body, Mending the Mind; The Power of the Mind to Heal*

Chopra, Deepak, M.D., *Quantum Healing; Unconditional Life; Ageless Body, Timeless Mind*

Dossey, Larry, M.D., *Healing Words; Prayer is Good Medicine*

Hay, Louise, *Heal Your Body*

Murphy, Michael, *The Future of the Body*

Northrup, Christine, M.D., *Women's Bodies, Women's Health*

Orloff, Judith, M.D., *Second Sight*

Page, Linda, N.D., Ph.D. *Healthy Healing*

Rossman, Martin, M.D., *Healing Yourself*

Virtue, Doreen, *Losing Your Pounds of Pain*

Siegel, Bernie, M.D., *Love, Medicine, and Miracles;*
Peace, Love, and Healing

Simonton, O. Carl, M.D., *Getting Well Again;*
The Healing Journey

Weil, Andrew, M.D., *Spontaneous Healing;*
8 Weeks to Optimum Health

PROSPERITY, SUCCESS, AND CAREER

Butterworth, Eric, *Spiritual Economics*

Chopra, Deepak, M.D., *Seven Spiritual Laws of Success;*
Creating Abundance

Cota–Robles, Patricia, *Take Charge of Your Life*

Johnson, Spencer, M.D., *Who Moved My Cheese?*

Laut, Phil, *Money is My Friend*

Orman, Suze, *The Nine Steps to Financial Freedom*

Ponder, Catherine, *Opening Your Mind to Prosperity*

Price, John Randolph, *The Abundance Book;*
The Success Book

Robinson, Jonathon, *Real Wealth*

Roman, Sanaya and Packer, Duane, *Creating Money*

Sinetar, Marsha, *Do What You Love, The Money Will Follow*

RELATIONSHIPS

Chopra, Deepak, M.D., *The Path to Love*

Gawain, Shakti, *Return to the Garden*

Hendricks, Gay and Kathleen, *Conscious Loving;*
The Conscious Heart

Hendrix, Hardville, *Getting the Love You Want*

Jeffers, Susan, Ph.D., *Opening Our Hearts to Men*

Keyes, Ken, *A Conscious Person's Guide to Relationships*

Stone, Hal, Ph.D., and Sidra, Ph.D., *Embracing Each Other*

Welwood, John, *Journey of the Heart*

Audio Tapes for Meditation and Guided Imagery

Crane, Patricia, Ph.D., *Inner Balance, Outer Harmony;*
Sunrise, Sunset; Peaceful Meditations;
Meditation: The Basics

Crane, Patricia, Ph.D. and Nichols, Rick, *Healthy, Wealthy, and*
Wise; Mind, Body, Miracles!

Dyer, Wayne, *Meditations for Manifestation*

Gawain, Shakti, *Creative Visualization Meditations*

Nichols, Rick, *Colors of Spirit*

Workshops

Patricia and her partner Rick Nichols lead workshops and training programs on the principles in this book throughout the world. To sponsor a workshop or be on their mailing list, please call (760) 728–8783, email them at patricia@heartinspired.com, or write to P.O. Box 1081, Bonsall, CA 92003. For current programs and to order any of their tapes or another copy of this book, please go to their website, www.heartinspired.com.

To further your study with the concepts in this book, Patricia and Rick have created several powerful on-line courses for self-paced study. Please go to www.changeinsideout.com for these courses.

For a list of workshop leaders worldwide trained by Patricia, please go to: www.hylteachers.com.

More Cosmic Kitchen Stories

If you have a story about how you used the techniques in this book to manifest something in your life and would like to have that story considered for inclusion in a future book, please submit it to either the post office address or email address listed above.

About the author.....

    For over 20 years Patricia has been designing and leading workshops on the principles in this book. Her own personal journey to reduce stress, increase balance, and discover the meaning and purpose of life began in the early 1970's. Her search led her to the techniques in this book.

    Patricia's Ph.D. is in social psychology with a specialty focus on wellness programs in the workplace. For several years she taught stress management courses at the university level and gave corporate workshops. Her studies in body–mind–spirit include *A Course in Miracles* and attending many of Marianne Williamson's lectures, books and workshops with Louise Hay and Deepak Chopra, M.D., Reiki Natural Healing, Transformational Breath, Science of Mind philosophy, and much more. She has given hundreds of talks and workshops on meditation, inner child work, the mind–body connection, Reiki Natural Healing, and using affirmations and visualizations to create what you want in life. She has also produced and recorded several meditation/relaxation tapes.

    Her intention is to continue sharing a message of personal empowerment in co–creation with Spirit. Patricia is committed to the expansion of the heart for personal and planetary healing.